WONDERS OF NATURE

A CHILD'S INTRODUCTION
TO THE WORLD OF ANIMALS, PLANTS,
BIRDS, FISH & INSECTS

Published By
PARENTS' MAGAZINE PRESS

A division of
Parents' Magazine Enterprises, Inc.
New York, N.Y.

1974

Parents' Magazine Enterprises, Inc.

From: Children's Guide To Knowledge (Chap. 1-8)
Copyright MCMLXIII, Parents' Magazine Enterprises, Inc.
Library of Congress Catalog Card No. 63-11929

Manufactured in the United States of America

CONTENTS

Pets

Terriers
Long-Legged Terriers
Short-Legged Terriers
Beagles
Greyhounds
Spaniels
Boxers
St. Bernards
Collies
German Shepherds
Police Dogs
Setters
Pekingese
Poodles
Great Danes
Doberman Pinschers
Dalmatians
Eskimo Dogs
Pomeranians
Tabby Cats
Persians
Maine
Siamese
Burmese
Maltese
Abyssinians
Manx
Bird Pets
Talking Birds
Singing Birds
Fishes
Caged Pets
Hamsters
Guinea Pigs
White Mice
Rabbits

THE first animals men knew were the wild ones they caught to eat. But while they were hunting for their food, another wild animal that hunted along with them became their closest friend. This was the wild dog.

The wild dogs were faster than men, and could see farther and smell farther, so their help was welcome. But men had learned to make arrows and spears and stone knives to kill the food animals, and when it came time to eat men built a fire. The dogs curled up by the fire, and shared the food they had helped to catch. By these forest fireplaces dogs and men became friends.

Dogs were the first pets. Pets are special kinds of tame animals that are kept not because they are useful, for food or their wool or skins, or because they help in farm work, but because they are fun to have around. Of course many pets are helpful to their owners. Dogs herd sheep and cattle, help the police, and guide the blind. Cats catch mice. But dogs and cats are also wonderful companions. Later, people found that even mice and birds and fish and rabbits were fun. So all these became pets.

TERRIERS

AIREDALE

THERE are several different breeds of Terrier. They were originally called "earth dogs" (that is what Terrier means), and were used to catch small animals.

Now Terriers are mostly housedogs, and they make fine guardians, because they bark fiercely if an unwelcome stranger comes near. There are long-legged and short-legged kinds.

LONG-LEGGED TERRIERS

THE Airedale is a long-legged Terrier about two feet high and usually colored tan. Bull Terriers, usually white, are the strongest dogs for their weight, and yet they are noted for their gentleness. One dog of this kind, finding it had to fight a tiny Pekingese which teased it, picked the little fellow up and placed it gently in a waste basket.

Fox Terriers, both smooth and wire-haired, are gay, brave, loyal, and lovely to look at. Other long-legged Terriers are the Irish, the Welsh, and the Bedlington.

SCOTTIE

WIREHAIRED
TERRIER

SHORT-LEGGED
TERRIERS

THE best known short-legged Terriers are the Scotties. They are shaggy. often black or sand-colored, with small pointed ears and erect tails. Sealyham and Dandie Dinmonts are other short-legged Terriers.

Many Terriers have lived in the White House, among them Theodore Roosevelt's Scamp, Woodrow Wilson's Davie, Calvin Coolidge's Peter Pan, and Franklin D. Roosevelt's Fala.

FOX TERRIER

BEAGLES

THE Beagle is a merry dog, about a foot high, with a short coat of no special color—it can be black-and-white, tan, or a combination. The Beagle is really a kind of hound, and its notion of a good time is to chase rabbits across a rough field.

No dog is more gentle and affectionate than the Beagle, especially if it is treated with kindness. But the kindest thing you can do is to be sure it gets out for a good run ever so often!

GREYHOUNDS

GREYHOUNDS are swift dogs with long, narrow heads. They are not always grey, in spite of their name. They were used for hunting as long as 6,000 years ago. Now they are used as pets and in dog racing.

SPANIELS

SPANIELS get their name from Spain, where they were bred 700 years ago. Spaniels enjoy retrieving because they are really hunting dogs, long trained to find and bring back birds that hunters have shot. Some Spaniels like water so much that they are called Water Spaniels. Cocker Spaniels have their name because they were used to help hunt woodcocks.

BOXERS

BOXERS are big dogs, up to two feet high, with faces somewhat like bulldogs. They are very gentle and intelligent, and are even used as Seeing-Eye Dogs.

Boxers have smooth coats of lovely yellow-brown, called fawn, or a sort of gray color with dark spots, called brindle. Their eyes are somewhat thoughtful, but never worried. No one knows why they are called Boxers, but it is not because they fight.

ST. BERNARDS

THIS powerful dog, with an uncanny sense of direction, was originally bred by monks in the St. Bernard region of Switzerland. St. Bernards rescue people lost in the snow drifts of the Swiss Alps. During the past 300 years, they have saved the lives of more than 2,500 persons.

COLLIES

COLLIES are big, shaggy dogs with long silky coats and long lean heads. Their eyes are very gentle, and they often seem to be smiling. They are often named "Laddie" or "Lassie," and everyone knows the famous film star by that name!

Collies came originally from Scotland, where they were used to tend the sheep, and they are still used more than most dogs for farm work. Yet Collies are favorite house and pet dogs. They are kind, loyal, and able to learn very difficult tricks.

GERMAN SHEPHERDS

LIKE the Collie, the German Shepherd was originally trained as a sheep dog. It is about two feet high, noble and fearless in appearance, with a rough coat any color from black to gray. German Shepherds are very loyal to their masters.

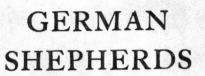

POLICE DOGS

GERMAN Shepherds are also called Police Dogs, because they can be trained to help the police track down criminals.

German Shepherds are the most loved of all dogs by the blind. As Seeing-Eye Dogs, they lead their sightless masters through crowded streets and into buses and subway trains, where no other dog is allowed.

14

SETTERS

THE Setter is a dog that loves the outdoors, and needs plenty of exercise. There are several kinds, and they are all known for their beauty and gentleness. The English Setter looks something like a Spaniel, and is one of the foremost of hunting dogs. The Irish Setter is always a golden red and hunts when it can, but because of its beauty it is often bred for dog shows.

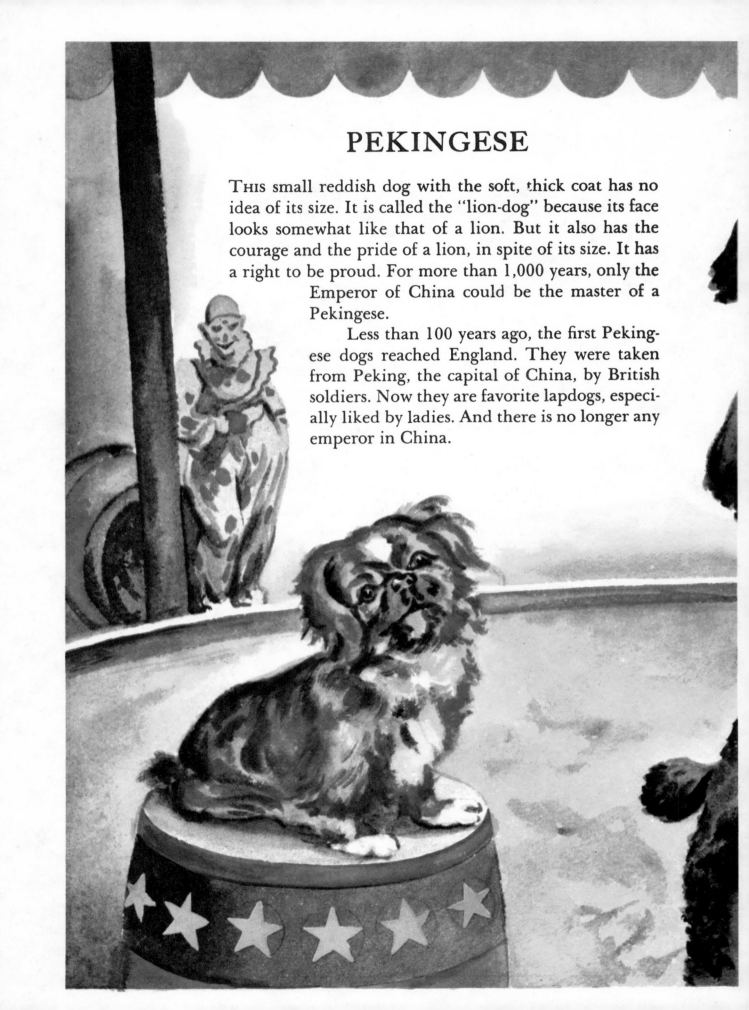

PEKINGESE

THIS small reddish dog with the soft, thick coat has no idea of its size. It is called the "lion-dog" because its face looks somewhat like that of a lion. But it also has the courage and the pride of a lion, in spite of its size. It has a right to be proud. For more than 1,000 years, only the Emperor of China could be the master of a Pekingese.

Less than 100 years ago, the first Pekingese dogs reached England. They were taken from Peking, the capital of China, by British soldiers. Now they are favorite lapdogs, especially liked by ladies. And there is no longer any emperor in China.

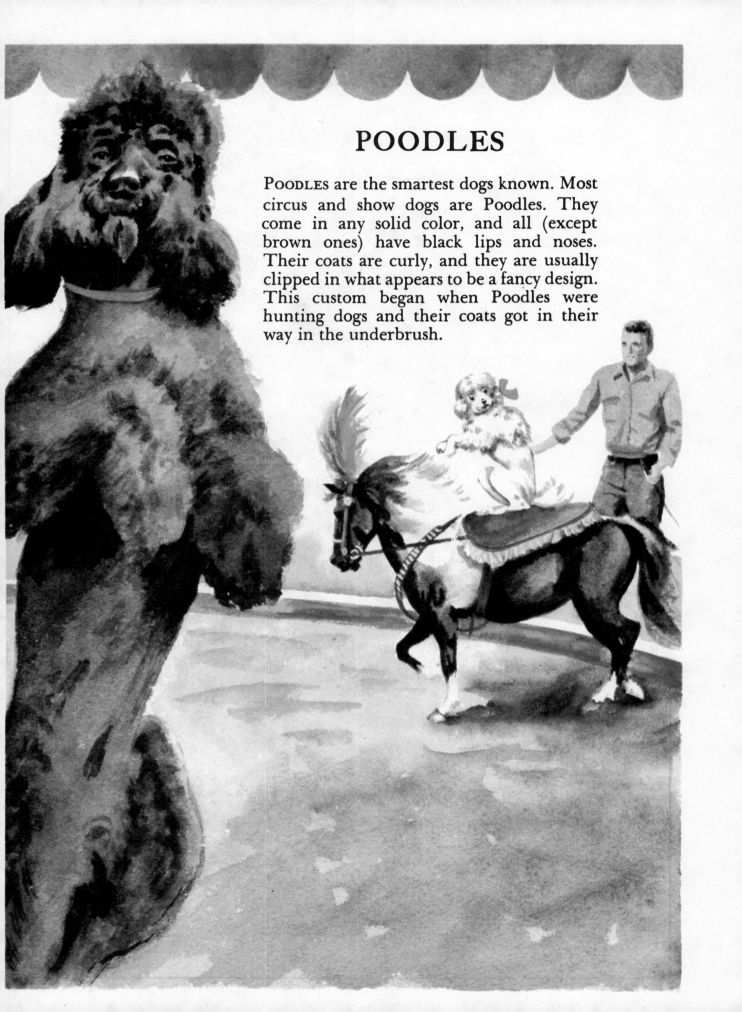

POODLES

POODLES are the smartest dogs known. Most circus and show dogs are Poodles. They come in any solid color, and all (except brown ones) have black lips and noses. Their coats are curly, and they are usually clipped in what appears to be a fancy design. This custom began when Poodles were hunting dogs and their coats got in their way in the underbrush.

GREAT DANES

GREAT Danes are three feet tall and have short, thick coats. No other dog stands as proudly. It is one of the oldest known breeds, for its picture was painted by Egyptian artists 4,000 years ago.

DOBERMAN PINSCHERS

DOBERMANN, a German dog lover, made up his mind to breed a terrier (Pinscher in German) so that it would be the size of a shepherd dog. The dog that resulted is brave, intelligent, and obedient. It is a fine police dog and is used as a Seeing-Eye Dog.

DALMATIANS

MANY fire-houses have Dalmatians as mascots. These big white dogs, with black or brown spots, love horses and are also fine watch dogs. They are loyal, brave, and friendly, and they make wonderful pets.

19

ESKIMO DOGS

In the cold northern regions of America live the Eskimos and their dogs, which are named after them. These dogs are not really pets. They are seldom even allowed to enter an Eskimo house, or igloo. But they are certainly helpful to everyone in the northland, because they pull the sleds hundreds of miles over the snow and ice, and can always find their way home, even when their masters are lost.

POMERANIANS

A COUSIN of the Eskimo Dog is the small, fluffy, gentle Pomeranian. This breed owes its popularity to one woman, Queen Victoria of England, who bought one in Florence and brought it back home.

Queen Victoria's pet weighed about 30 pounds. But the Pomeranian that is carried from home to home today weighs no more than seven pounds. This is the result of breeding, that is, of always picking the smallest puppies to be the parents of the next family.

TABBY CATS

ALL cats are soft, cuddly, and willing to purr when they are happy. They come in many colors and shapes, with long or short hair. Cats are called independent because, unlike dogs, they only love their owners when they are treated with love and understanding. But they really depend on their owners just as dogs do.

Most cats belong to no breed at all, but are mixtures of several breeds. Such cats are often striped, and are called Tabby cats. Their name comes from a kind of striped or wavy cloth called "attabi" by the Arabs.

PERSIANS
AND MAINE CATS

ALL cats probably came from the East, and those with long hair are called Persians. The kittens are fluffy and will grow up with the same color—snow white, creamy white, coppery red, dusky blue, tortoise-shell (a kind of brown

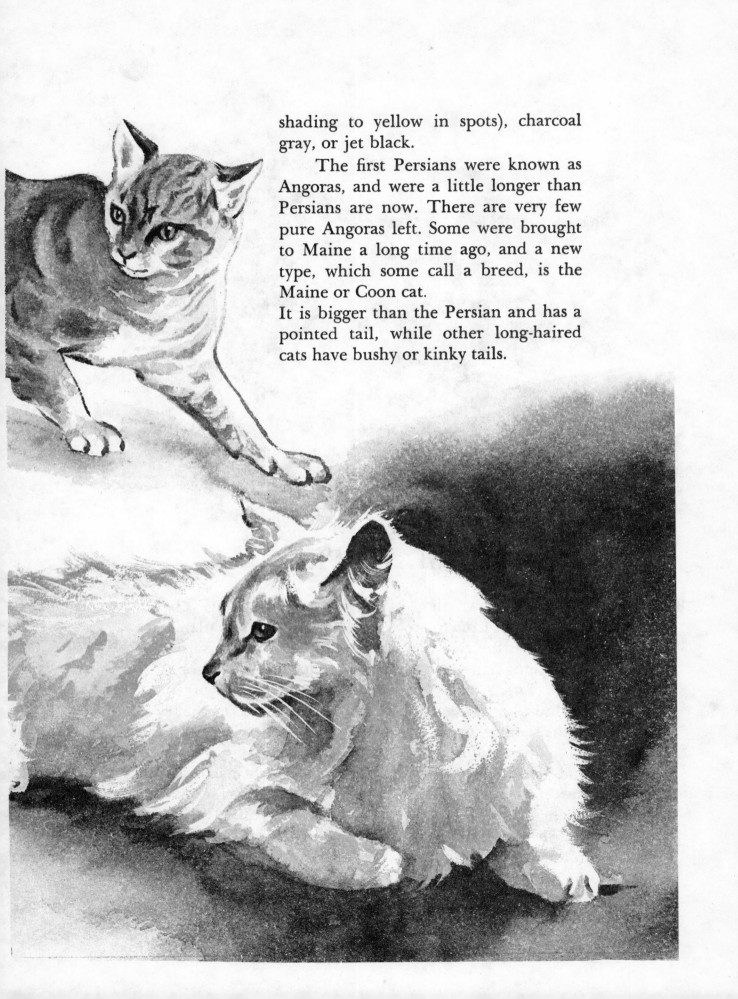

shading to yellow in spots), charcoal gray, or jet black.

The first Persians were known as Angoras, and were a little longer than Persians are now. There are very few pure Angoras left. Some were brought to Maine a long time ago, and a new type, which some call a breed, is the Maine or Coon cat.
It is bigger than the Persian and has a pointed tail, while other long-haired cats have bushy or kinky tails.

SIAMESE

The best known short-haired cat is the Siamese. This breed comes from Siam (which is now called Thailand), where it is the common housecat. They are not as fluffy as the long-haired cats, and their color often changes. A white kitten may become a light-brown (fawn) or shadow-blue cat, and it will usually have darker shades of the same color on its face, legs, and tail.

The eyes of Siamese cats are almost always blue, and often they are crossed, but this does not mean that they have poor sight. All cats have very keen sight, even when the light is dim. You can see how much bigger their eyes are at dusk or by firelight. But cats cannot see in total darkness, as many people believe.

24

BURMESE

BURMA is a country near Thailand where the Siamese cats came from. Burmese cats also have short hair and long bodies, but their colors and eyes are different. Most Burmese kittens are light brown which becomes deeper as they grow. They have round eyes, colored greenish or yellowish.

MAINE

(See page 22.)

ABYSSINIAN

MALTESE

MANX, MALTESE, ABYSSINIANS

THE Abyssinian cat has fur that is more like that of a rabbit than that of other breeds of cat. It is usually brown in color, with the tips a darker shade of brown, giving the cat an interesting speckly look. It has big ears, big eyes, and is very rare.

Manx cats are different from all others, because they have no tails at all. Their hind legs are higher than their front legs, so they look like rabbits when they run. They are usually striped, either blue or brown, or solid black or white, and their heads are rather large. Real Manx cats are so rare that sometimes dishonest cat dealers cut the tails from other breeds of cat and sell them as Manx cats.

Maltese cats are beautiful blue cats of no special breed, just like Tabbies.

MANX

27

BIRD PETS

MANY kinds of birds can be tamed and kept in cages. There you can take good care of them. They would not be happy if they were free, like other birds, because they would not know how to take care of themselves.

TALKING BIRDS

SOME birds have voices that are almost human. By listening to human speech they can learn to talk, too. Of course, they do not know what they are saying, and they will never say anything they have not heard someone else say many times over.

Parrakeets are the most popular of talking birds. They have beautiful feathers of many bright colors, green and blue and yellow.

SINGING BIRDS

THE tame bird with the finest singing voice is the beautiful Canary, which is usually yellow. A Canary sings best when it is happy. Whistle or sing to it, and see if it does not answer.

FISHES

A PET fish is no tamer than any other fish, but it is more beautiful. Goldfish are kept in bowls where you can watch them as they dart about. At feeding time, you tap the bowl and they understand. Another pet fish is the Guppy.

CAGED PETS

Some pet animals are so small that they would get lost or hurt if they were allowed to be free, so they are kept in cages. These cages are their homes. After they know you well enough to go out for a short time, they will come back to their cages and sleep or play there.

HAMSTERS

The first Hamsters were brought here from Europe in the 1930's. These furry animals are only about six inches long. They have pointed noses and round ears and pouches in their cheeks where they store food to eat later. They love to be petted.

GUINEA PIGS

Guinea Pigs are not pigs at all, and they do not come from the country of Guinea, but from South America where they were tamed by the Indians. They are about six inches long, with chunky bodies of various colors, pointed faces, and no tails at all. They are very gentle and talk by squeaking.

WHITE MICE

White Mice are often kept as pets because they are so pretty and lively. If their cage has a tiny trapeze, such as acrobats use, they will learn to swing on it. They must always be kept in their cages.

RABBITS

SOME Rabbits are white and silky, with broad floppy ears. Others have small, perky ears and short hair. Rabbits love to be cuddled, and to play games. If they are annoyed, they show it by knocking their hind legs against the floor.

Cats may learn to play with Rabbits, but some dogs never learn this because they are trained to hunt hares, which look like Rabbits. Every Rabbit likes to have its own comfortable home which should be built like a wild Rabbit's burrow.

Domestic Animals

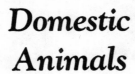

Aberdeen Angus
Brahman
Holstein and Jersey
Cayuse
Bucephalus
A Knight's Horse
Percherons
Mustang and Bronco
Quarter Horse
Ponies
Donkeys
Mules
Sheep
Goats
Angora
Cashmere
Pigs
Chickens
Ducks
Geese
Turkeys
Fur Bearing Animals

Aberdeen Angus and Brahman

THE very best cattle are bred to provide either beef or milk, not both.

A fine beef-producing breed is the Aberdeen-Angus, a coal-black animal that comes from the highlands of Scotland. These cattle are much smaller than the silver-gray Brahmans, which are brought all the way from India. Brahmans are usually mated to cattle of other breeds, and in this way a new breed is formed.

Holstein and Jersey

THE black-and-white Holstein and the brown Jersey are two of the best dairy cows. They are raised mainly for the milk they produce. The Holstein provides more milk each day, but the Jersey provides milk that is creamier.

Of course, dairy cows also produce calves. Male calves are not usually allowed to grow up. They are turned into meat, which is very tender and is called veal. Female calves are called heifers until they grow up and become cows. On farms, children often choose a pretty heifer to become a pet.

Cayuse

THE Cayuse is still seen in the West and, of course, in the movies. It is a strong, yet active animal, able to cover difficult ground at a rapid rate without getting too tired. The famous Pony Express was carried by these small horses, bringing the mail across mountains and deserts before the railroads were built. They are also called Mustangs, but the name Cayuse is most often used. Their ancestors were the wild horses of the plains. And there is no horse that brings back the memory of the Old West in the way the Cayuse does, especially when an Indian is in the saddle.

Bucephalus

LONG ago there was a tiny kingdom called Macedonia. The King was buying horses one day. One horse seemed so wild that the King refused to buy him. But the King's son, Prince Alexander, made friends with the black beauty, whose name was Bucephalus, and tamed him.

When Alexander became king, he conquered the world, and wherever he went he rode on Bucephalus. After Bucephalus died, Alexander built a new city and named it Bucephala.

A Knight's Horse

IN olden times every knight had his horse, cared for by a squire. It was a beautiful, strong animal, but not nearly so fast as our race horses today. It had to be strong to carry the weight of the armor as well as the rider.

When the knights from Europe fought battles against the horsemen from Asia, the knights were sometimes beaten because their horses were too slow. The horsemen from Asia used fast Arabian animals, more like our race horses.

Percherons

THE Percheron is one of the most famous of work horses. It was brought here from France, and its ancestors were the sturdy horses of the knights and the lighter Arabian horses. For hundreds of years Percherons and other strong horses did heavy farm work and pulled coaches or carts. Now the Percherons are vanishing, because machines have taken their places.

Mustang and Bronco

Horses first came to America with Columbus. These were called Barbs because they had originally come from the Barbary coast of Africa.

Soon there were Barbs on every ranch in Spanish Mexico. When the Indians captured many of these ranches, the horses escaped. The Barbs wandered wild all over the West for hundreds of years. When the cowboys reached the Far West they caught and tamed these horses.

The cowboys called them Mustangs. Before a Mustang is "broken" or tamed, it is often called a Bronco.

40

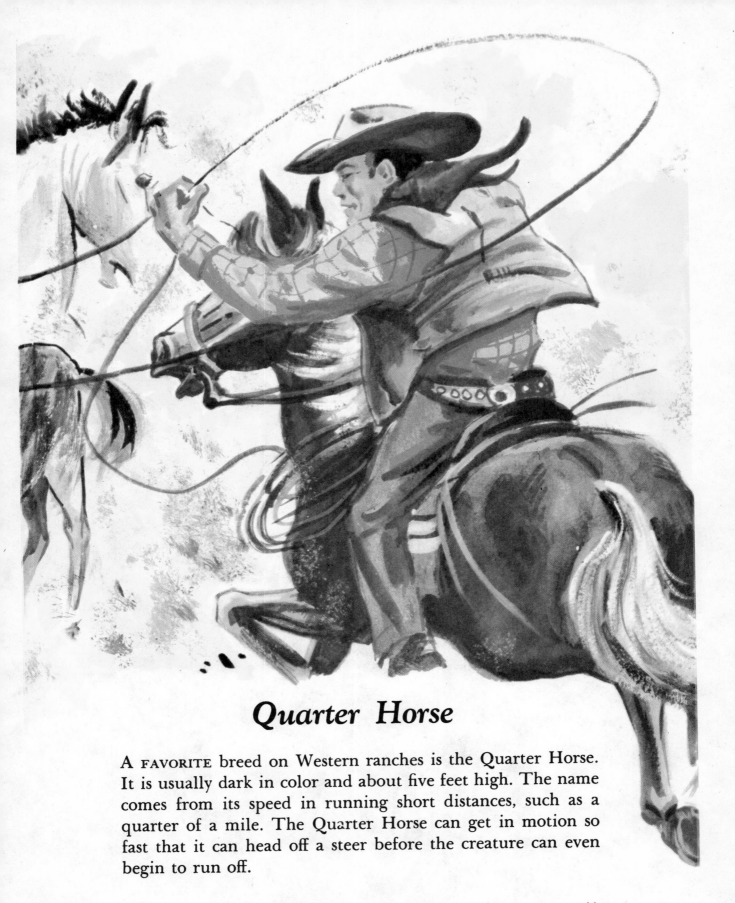

Quarter Horse

A FAVORITE breed on Western ranches is the Quarter Horse. It is usually dark in color and about five feet high. The name comes from its speed in running short distances, such as a quarter of a mile. The Quarter Horse can get in motion so fast that it can head off a steer before the creature can even begin to run off.

Ponies

PONIES are really small horses of special breeds. Shetland ponies, the most popular, are about 40 inches high. They may be black, brown, or spotted, and they have two coats, a summer coat that is short and glossy, and a shaggy winter coat that comes off in the spring.

Shetland ponies are fine pets, just big enough for a child to ride or drive. They are usually gentle, but some of them can become stubborn at times.

Donkeys

A COUSIN of the horse is the donkey, also called an ass. (If it is male, it is called a jackass.) In spite of its reputation, the donkey is not stupid. It is about the size of a pony, has short hair, and long ears.

In Mexico and South America, donkeys called burros are used to carry heavy loads.

Mules

IF a jackass is mated to a female horse (a mare), the young ones will be mules. They are hard workers, but sometimes they just refuse to work. Then they become "as stubborn as a mule."

43

Sheep

IN ancient Greece, they told how a hero named Jason sailed to the end of the world to find a treasure called the Golden Fleece. This is just a story, but all over the world farmers keep shy, gentle animals, with woolly coats which can be turned into money or gold. Only tame sheep have these coats. Wild sheep, such as the Rocky Mountain Bighorns, have no wool.

The best wool sheep, Merinos, came from Spain, where the king tried to keep them. But many of them were brought out — Cortes brought some to America—and now Merinos are found all over the world. They produce very fine wool, especially a French type of Merino called the Rambouillet.

In England, they learned to breed sheep like the Lincoln which have very long wool, others like the Hampshire and Dorset which have poor wool but good meat, and still others like the Corriedale which produce wool and meat. The meat of sheep is delicious, as you know, for surely you enjoy lamb chops.

Sheep like to roam over grassland. When they have finished eating, the grass looks as though it had been freshly cut. Often more than 1,000 sheep are guarded in one flock by a herder and his dogs.

Goats

GOATS are like sheep in many ways. All goats have horns, as do many sheep, but the horns of sheep are shaped like a corkscrew, while those of goats fork up and out.

Male goats, called billy-goats, have beards. Female goats, called nanny-goats, are fine milk producers. Their milk is saved for children and sick people who cannot drink cow's milk.

Angora

GOATS have fleece, which is not called wool, but mohair. It is long and silky, and cannot mat. or felt, as wool can. The best fleece-producing goat in this country is the Angora which was first bred in Turkey.

The Angora is smaller than a sheep or a milk goat. It has long ears, horns often more than two feet long, and a noble expression.

Cashmere

FLEECE finer than that of any sheep comes from a goat found only in the valley of Kashmir, in India. Both the goat and the fleece, which is often called wool, have the name of this valley, but spelled differently—Cashmere.

Pigs

Pigs are heavy, thick-skinned animals with short legs, almost no neck at all, and a long snout. They are neither lazy nor dirty, but they do love to roll in mud, just as a dog loves to roll in grass.

Before a pig is a year old it will weigh 200 pounds. Then it is ready to be turned into tasty ham and bacon.

Some pigs are fed corn until they cannot eat any more.

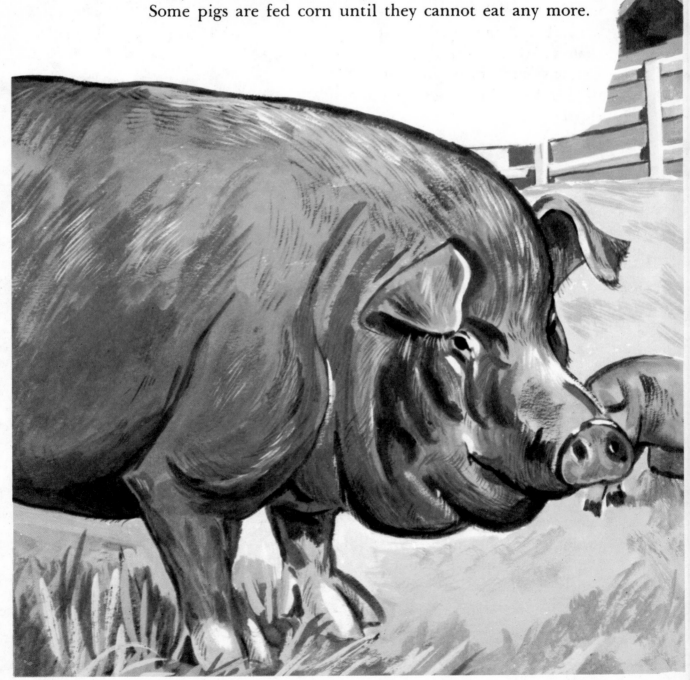

They grow into hogs, weighing as much as 1,000 pounds, and they are very fat. This pleases the farmer, because all the fat on these hogs is valuable. It is turned into lard, which is used for cooking. Other parts of the animal are also useful. Strong leather is made of pigskin, and the tough hairs, called bristles, are made into brushes.

49

Chickens

In the jungles of Asia, there is a large bird with brilliant colors—red feathers on the wings, yellow on the neck and head, black on the tail. It is hard to believe that our common chicken is related to this jungle bird, but it is the same animal, except that the chicken is tame.

Almost all farmers raise some chickens, and some raise nothing else. Imagine the noise they must make, all cackling at once! Chickens provide delicious meat and billions of eggs every year.

Chickens cannot fly very high or very far. They eat by picking at their feed with their strong beaks. The little chicks are very lively.

Most American chickens are kept for both meat and eggs. The best egg chicken is the Leghorn, from Italy. If its ear lobes are white, the eggs it lays will be white too, but if the ear lobes are red, it will lay brown eggs. Both are good to eat.

A chicken farm is very noisy, because chickens make all kinds of sounds. The happiest sound comes after an egg has been laid, and the loudest comes early in the morning, when the roosters (male chickens) wake everyone with their crowing.

51

Ducks

DUCKS are tame water-birds that sleep on land, but their short legs and webbed feet are not much good for walking. In the water, however, they get along fine, and as soon as they come out their feathers are dry. A mother duck gliding through the water, followed by all the little ducklings, is a pretty sight.

Farmers breed ducks for their fine meat. Long Island, in New York, is famous for its tasty ducklings. The most popular breeds are white.

Geese

A COUSIN of the duck is the goose. Its neck and legs are longer than those of a duck, but its feet are webbed and it is at home in the water.

Geese are good to eat, but the best part of all is the liver which is chopped up to make a spread. Goose feathers, which are very soft, are used for stuffing pillows.

Tame geese are gray or white. When a goose wants to talk, it makes a single loud noise, a honk, that sounds like a rusty automobile horn.

Turkeys

TURKEYS are as American as Thanksgiving, when they are almost always served for dinner. The Indians had learned to tame these big, bright-feathered birds. The Spaniards who came over after Columbus discovered America took turkeys back home, and some of them reached England. Then the Pilgrims brought a few of them back to America on the Mayflower. They must have been surprised to find wild turkeys all through the New England woods.

Turkeys, wild or tame, are beautiful birds because of their brilliant colors — green, golden, coppery in some types, although there are plain white ones too. One famous type is called the Bronze, another the Bourbon Red. They are much larger than chickens, and their meat is very solid.

You cannot be hungry after a turkey dinner. Many years ago, when families were larger, with a dozen children and sometimes more, one turkey would be just enough for a good meal. But now, few families could finish eating such a big bird, so the turkey farmers have learned to breed new types that weigh little more than a large chicken.

Fur-Bearing Animals

THE last animals to be raised on farms were those which are valued for their fur. Although they live in man-made homes, they never become tame, and are not pets.

The silver fox was the first animal to be kept on fur farms. Its fur is really black with hairs tipped gray or white, giving the coat a frosty look.

The mink is small, with soft brown fur. Hundreds of minks are needed to make one garment.

The chinchilla is like a squirrel, so small you can hold it in your hand. Its fur is soft and gray and thick. Chinchillas originally came from South America, but so many were killed that they became rare. Now some are raised on farms.

Wild Animals

Mongoose

THE Mongoose is a famous snake killer. Although only two feet long, it will attack a poisonous snake seven feet long. It is found in Africa and Asia, where there are many snakes. Sometimes the Mongoose gets bitten by a snake, but this does not happen often.

Aardvark

AARDVARK is a South African Dutch name which means earth pig. The Aardvark does look a little like a pig but it is not really a pig.

The Aardvark sleeps in a hole during the day. At night it comes out to look for termites. With its sharp claws, it easily tears open the termite mounds. And with its long, sticky tongue, it licks along the opened mound, gobbling up the termites.

Anteater

THE Anteater lives in swampy forests in Central and South America. The animal's long head comes to a point at the end of its mouth.

The Anteater has no teeth. Its tongue is almost two feet long, and sticky, so it can lick up ants. It uses the long powerful claws on its front feet to dig up large ant hills.

Giant Armadillo

THE Giant Armadillo lives in the jungles of South America. It has a hard protective covering over its head and body, which looks a lot like the armor that knights of the Middle Ages used to wear in battle.

59

Cougar

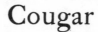

THE animal shown leaping through the air on the left side of the picture is a Cougar, or Puma. It is sometimes called a Panther. A member of the cat family, the Cougar is native to America. The Cougar can leap as many as 20 feet with ease, and 60-foot leaps have been recorded.

Jaguar

THE spotted Jaguar, shown in the lower part of the picture, is the most powerful of all the wild cats in America.

Many Jaguars live in the jungles of South America. There the owners of cattle ranches hire professional hunters to hunt the Jaguars, because these animals prey on defenseless cattle.

Cheetah

THE Cheetah of Africa and India is one of the swiftest four-legged animals in the world. Its speed has been officially timed at 48 miles an hour, but some people claim to have seen it travel at 70 miles an hour.

Hippopotamus

HIPPOPOTAMUS is a Greek word that means river horse, but the Hippopotamus is really related to the pig. It has a very large round body and short legs. It lives in Africa, in the same waters as the crocodile, but the two animals do not bother each other. When the Hippopotamus swims, only its eyes and nose stick up out of the water.

The Hippopotamus can close its nose like a bottle cap and stay under water for as long as 30 minutes. When it comes up and opens its nose with a loud snort, a foot-high spray of water shoots out. The Hippopotamus lives on vegetables.

Rhinoceros

A VERY large, clumsy animal is the Rhinoceros. It has one and sometimes two horns on its head between the nose and eyes. This animal is very short-sighted and bad tempered. Perhaps this is why it often charges without any reason.

In India there is a belief that a Rhinoceros horn has magical powers. Some natives think that drinking from the horn will keep a person from becoming poisoned. If he is already poisoned, they think it will cure him.

Buffalo

THE Buffalo once roamed all over the North American plains.
There were millions of Buffaloes in a single herd. The American Buffalo is also known as the Bison. India is the home of
the Water Buffalo. The Cape Buffalo comes from Africa. The
Bison is a big powerful animal. There is thick hair around its
head and neck and shoulders and a black beard on its chin.

The Bison was a very important animal in the history of
America. It was killed for food and clothing by the Indians and
the early white settlers. Buffalo Bill was a famous hunter of
Buffaloes or Bison. He was hired by the Kansas Pacific Railroad,
in 1876, to kill the Buffaloes to keep them away from the railroad tracks. So many were killed that today, there are only a few
thousand Buffaloes left.

Deer

DEER inhabit almost every region of the world. We speak of the adult male of most species of deer as a buck. The adult female is called a doe. The fawn is a young deer.

The antlers of male deer are those hard bones that grow from the head and look like tree branches. At the end of every mating season, these antlers fall off, but new ones grow the next year. The Moose is the largest of the deer. Caribou is the common name for our North American Reindeer. Do you remember the names of the eight Reindeer in the lovely poem, "Visit from St. Nicholas"?

Elephant

THE largest animal that lives on land is the Elephant. The African Elephant grows as tall as 12 feet and may weigh as much as 12 tons. The Elephant uses the long snout, called a trunk, to eat leaves from trees, to drink water, and to bathe itself. It also uses the trunk to scent enemies because its eyesight is very poor. The trunk is strong enough to pull up large trees.

We all know how big the Elephant's ears are. The strange thing is that the Elephant cannot hear too well. The Elephant is astonishingly smart. Once, a herd of Elephants came to a stream which was too shallow to bathe in. All the Elephants started building a dam across the stream. The dam blocked up the water and made a fine deep pool for bathing.

66

Waterbuck

THE Waterbuck on the right of this picture belongs to the antelope family. Its home is in Africa. It is really a land animal. But whenever it is frightened it hides in the water. The Waterbuck is a good swimmer.

Gazelle

THE animal in the lower part of the picture above is the Gazelle. Only the cheetah can outrun it. The deserts of Africa and Asia are the Gazelle's home.

In 1946, newspapers printed a story about a boy who was brought up by Gazelles. Natives saw the boy running with Gazelles and caught him. A doctor said the boy acted just like a Gazelle. Some people thought the boy was left by his mother and the Gazelles found him.

Gibbon

THE Gibbon ape of Asia stands only about three feet high, but its arms are so long that its fingers touch the ground. The Gibbon walks with its hands over its head and looks as if it will fall forward on its face.

In the trees this ape swings easily from branch to branch. It has a loud voice and likes to scream while eating.

68

Orangutan

THE Orangutan's home is in Borneo and Sumatra. It leans on its knuckles when walking because of its very long arms. A captured Orangutan ape can be taught to ride a tricycle or to put on a suit.

69

Camel

No animal is better adapted to life in the desert than the Camel. When sandstorms blow, the Camel's eyes are shielded by its very long eyelashes. We all know that the Camel can go without water for days.

Do you think that water is stored in the humps of the Camel? Actually these humps store food, not water, as most people suppose. Inside the Camel's stomach are many pouches or sacks; that is where the water is stored. Sometimes, when desert travelers have no other water supply, they will cut open these sacks and drink the water as a last resort.

Rocky Mountain Goat

THE Rocky Mountain Goat is a little like a goat and a little like an antelope. It is not really either one. It has a thick white coat with horns that curve back. It lives on high mountain peaks. It is very sure-footed and very brave.

Wild Sheep

MANY years ago, all Sheep were wild, like the Angali of Asia. These are thought to be the ancestors of all tame Sheep. They have long, curled horns. Very much like them are the wild Bighorns of our Rocky Mountains. The wild Barbary Sheep of North Africa have shorter horns that do not curl.

71

Lion

We can certainly understand why the Lion has been named the King of the Beasts. The long flowing hair on its neck, called the mane, is wonderfully majestic looking. But the female Lion, or Lioness, does not have this long mane, and she does not look nearly so majestic.

Lions are the biggest members of the cat family. They sometimes weigh as much as 500 pounds. They are enormously powerful, always dangerous when they are hungry. Lions live in Africa and parts of India. They prefer the open country to the jungle.

Tiger

THE Tiger lives in regions of Asia that extend from cold Siberia all the way to hot India. There are no Tigers in Africa. The Tiger has a yellow-tan color with black stripes which hide it in the jungle. Tigers stalk their prey at night. Of all the cats, the Tiger is man's most dangerous enemy.

Leopard

THE Leopard's home is Africa. It is smaller than a lion or a tiger, but it is more ferocious. The Leopard has black spots in groups of five or six on its body. Sometimes it has so many black spots that it looks all black. The Leopard likes to stay around trees where it can hunt monkeys and birds.

Wolf

THE Wolf is a form of wild dog. Some people think it is the original ancestor of all our domestic dogs. Others think it is an altogether different breed. But we do know that Wolves can be tamed, and then they become as affectionate as the most affectionate domestic dog. Since they are very powerful, they are sometimes mated with sled-dogs, to make a stronger stock.

In the wild state, Wolves can be terribly vicious and destructive. They hunt in packs and will attack sheep and cattle. They make their homes in caves and in hollow tree trunks.

Jackal

THE Jackal is a wild dog that lives in Africa and Asia. Many people call the Jackal cowardly, because it usually attacks smaller animals or animals that have been wounded by others.

Fox

Do you know the sly, clever Fox in the Aesop and "Uncle Remus" stories? The Fox is famous for its cleverness, because of the amazing tricks it will play to escape from pursuers, like running through water or along the tops of fences so as not to leave behind tell-tale tracks.

The female Fox is called a vixen. When baby Foxes or cubs are born, they stay blind for ten days, like baby kittens. And, also like kittens, cubs love to chase each other.

Coyote

COYOTE is an Indian name for the Prairie Wolf. Coyotes hunt in packs at night, uttering the most blood-curdling howls. When they hunt jack-rabbits, Coyotes work in pairs. One gives chase, while the other waits and rests, knowing full well that jack-rabbits run in circles.

75

Kaola

THE Kaola of Australia looks just like a toy bear. It has no tail. A Kaola is a marsupial. A marsupial is an animal that holds its babies in a pouch on the outside of its stomach.

Kangaroo

ANOTHER native of Australia is the Kangaroo. It stands seven feet high. With its long back legs and long powerful tail, it can jump as far as 20 feet and hop along at 25 miles an hour.

Birds

IRDS, like people, have two legs, backbones, and warm blood. But instead of arms and hands, they have wings. They wear feathers in place of clothes. They lay eggs. The mother bird and sometimes the father bird, too, sit on the eggs to keep them warm, until the growing baby bird inside is big and strong enough to break the shell. Baby birds are almost as helpless as human babies. Their parents have to feed them and teach them how to fly.

Birds come in many sizes and in all the colors of the rainbow. The hummingbird's body is not much larger than the bowl of a tablespoon and it weighs less than the letter you drop in the mail box. But the ostrich grows eight and nine feet tall and weighs as much as two men.

The bird on this page is prehistoric. It lived many millions of years ago.

Ruby-Throated Hummingbird

THE smallest of all birds gets its name from the humming, motor-like sound of its beating wings. Like a helicopter, it can hover in one place and fly backwards. It can fly 70 miles an hour.

Whooping Crane

THE Whooping Crane is the tallest and loudest bird in North America. It is nearly five feet tall. When it whoops it can be heard all of three miles away. Usually, it lives for 50 years.

There used to be thousands upon thousands of Whooping Cranes in this country. Now there are nearly none left.

Blue Jay

FROM the tip of its beak to the tip of its tail, the Blue Jay is just a bit shorter than your 12-inch ruler. Blue Jays are very blue, very noisy, and great jokers.

On a hot summer afternoon, when owls like to sleep, several Blue Jays will gang up on a sleeping owl and awaken it with their brassy cries. Stealing acorns from squirrels is fun, too. Blue Jays gather and hide many more acorns and beechnuts than they can ever eat. But from these buried nuts forests of new trees have grown.

Strange as it seems, the beautiful Blue Jay is a cousin of the common crow. It is smaller and much more richly colored than the crow. Another Jay bird is the Robber Jay, so called because it steals food from hunters' camps.

Robin

THE Robin is the best known and best liked of all American birds. When the English settled in America they found large numbers of this member of the thrush family. They called it "Robin," because its red breast reminded them of the little English warbler called Robin they had left behind.

No American bird has adapted itself to modern civilization as well as the Robin. Today, it lives not only in villages and suburbs, but even in city parks and on the lawns of city houses. Unlike other migratory birds, it does not go all the way to South America in winter. It stops in Georgia and Florida. So the Robin is the first bird up north to hail the spring with its familiar call, "Cheer up, cheer up!"

Belted Kingfisher

Belted Kingfisher

THE Belted Kingfisher has wide stripes around the body that make it look like a barber shop pole. The males of most birds are richer or more gaudy looking than the females. The male of the Belted Kingfisher is an exception. But he makes up for it with a black crest that makes him look fierce.

The call of the Kingfisher is a harsh, rattling shriek.

Crested Flycatcher

Mockingbird

THE Mockingbird is the best singer and actor of all our birds. It will sing sweetly for hours on end, and then suddenly break off the song to imitate the song, whistle, or harsh calls of other birds.

It will imitate its cousin, the catbird, imitating a cat; and it will meow better than either of them. It will bark like a dog and has even been heard imitating the squeak of a garden gate's rusty hinge.

Mockingbird

Crested Flycatcher

THE Crested Flycatcher likes to fly after large insects and catch them in the air. It prefers to live in woodland country, but an old orchard will do. It will perch on a branch or railing for hours on end, waiting for some insect to fly by. Then it will dart quickly after the insect, snap it up, and return to its perch to wait for another insect.

The Crested Flycatcher's favorite nesting place is an empty woodpecker's hole. It will watch for a snake to shed its skin and will take the old skin to line its nest. If it cannot find any snakeskin, it will use onion skin and even man-made wax paper and cellophane. Its call is a long, loud wheeep!

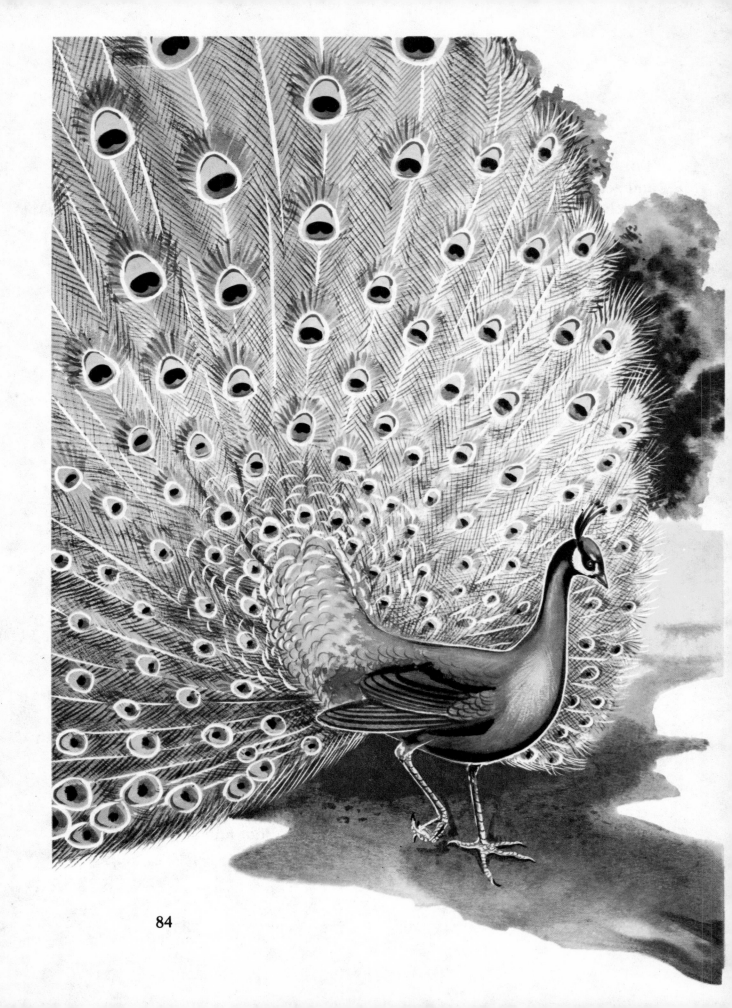

Peacock

THIS most gorgeous of all birds is a native of India and Ceylon. It still lives in large numbers in the jungles of Ceylon. It has been domesticated for centuries in Europe, and struts about the lawns and gardens of the rich, and in this democratic age, in public parks, too.

The male Peacock has a train of feathers from the lower part of his back and the upper part of his tail, which he can raise and open up like a huge fan of green and blue and gold. The Peacock does this to attract the female bird who has no such fan.

Great Blue Heron

THIS long-legged water bird is a beautiful steel blue, with white markings. Its feet are not webbed like the feet of a duck and many other water birds. Its separated toes are long enough for it to curve its feet around the branch of a tree and hold on.

It builds its nests in the trees that border the swamps of Florida, Louisiana, and Texas. Sometimes as many as 100,000 of these great Herons will nest in the same place. They will return to it each year. They live on fish, frogs, snakes, shrimps, crabs, and mice. In the summer they fly north but return to the south in the fall.

Starling

THE Starling is an immigrant. It used to live only in Europe, Asia and North Africa. It was first brought to New York City's Central Park, in 1890, to kill off insects that were destroying the trees. Today, there are many, many thousands of Starlings in this country.

The Starling loves company. It gathers in huge flocks that fly, without any apparent leader, in perfect and beautiful formations. It is very intelligent. It has been taught to whistle a tune and to speak a few words.

Red-Eyed Vireo

THE Red-Eyed Vireo's nest is so well built that it will last for several years. The Vireo is the victim of the lazy cowbird which sneaks its egg into the Vireo's nest. And the Vireo will sit on it, hatch, and bring up the young cowbird as if it were its own!

86

Tufted Titmouse

THE Tufted Titmouse is a perky, six-inch bird. The feathers on the top of its head stand up like the peak of an old fashioned nightcap. It does not go south in winter, but stays in swampy bottomlands.

It hunts for hidden insect eggs in the company of chickadees which belong to the Tit family, too. In summer its favorite food is caterpillars. This makes the Tufted Titmouse very popular with farmers. In winter as well as in spring and summer, the Tufted Titmouse is a loud and regular singer.

Long-Billed Marsh Wren

THIS little bird is not much larger than a hummingbird. The male usually has two or more wives. But these Wrens always build more nests than they have wives. Then, when attacked by big hawks or crows, the cagey male stands over the empty nest and chatters angrily at the attacker, while the wives sit quietly on their eggs or young ones.

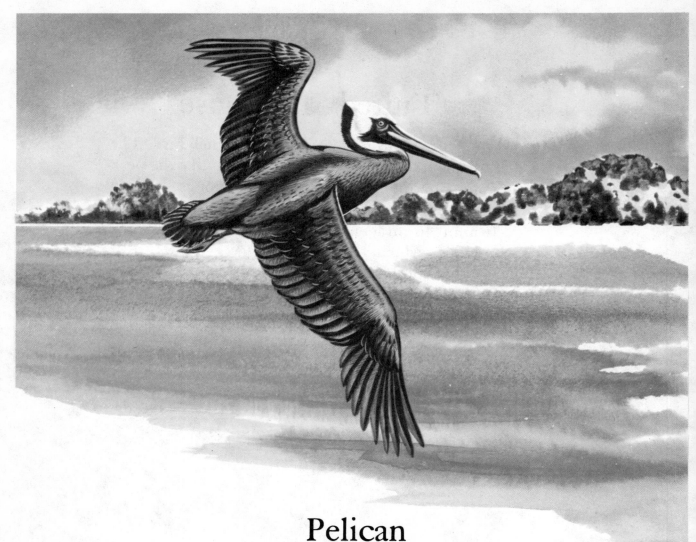

Pelican

HERE is a well-known saying about this peculiar bird:
> "There is an old bird called the Pelican
> Whose bill can hold more than his belly can.
> He can put in his beak
> Enough food for a week
> And I just don't see how well he can."

This is how the Pelican does it. Its bill is from nine to 13 inches long, and underneath the bill is a bag which is like a balloon with no air in it. This bag can be filled with food and stretched until it holds three and a half gallons! That is equal to 14 quarts of milk! The huge bill and the bag are used to scoop up water with fish in it. After making its dive, the Pelican raises its head high into the air. As the water flows out, the bag gets limp and small again and the fish slide down the Pelican's throat.

Flamingo

THIS vivid pink water bird is four feet tall from the tip of its bill to its toes. It breeds in the swamps of Louisiana and Florida.

The Flamingo does not build a nest in the trees or shrubs, as other birds do. But on the mud flats it builds a wide-bottomed, cup-shaped nest of clay and sticks, and lays its single egg in the center of this nest.

Sometimes, so many Flamingos build nests in the same place that they are called Flamingo cities. The birds stick their stubby, curved beaks into the mud and shallow water, and root out the shrimps and crabs they love to eat.

You might not think it, but ducks and geese are cousins of the Flamingo. The Flamingo makes a call that sounds like the deep honk-honk of many kinds of geese.

Condor

THIS is a South American vulture. It is the greatest and most powerful bird of prey in the world. It lives high in the Andes mountains of Peru and Chile. It flies higher than any mountain peaks in the United States.

The Condor never builds a nest but lays its eggs in saucer-shaped rocks. If very hungry, Condors will hunt in pairs, swooping down into the valley and carrying off a sheep, a deer, or some member of the llama family. Once plentiful, Condors today are very rare. Soon they will probably become extinct.

Roadrunner

ON dirt roads, from Kansas to California and south to Texas, you may see a funny-looking track with two toes pointing forward and two backward. They were made by the Roadrunner, a bird that can run as fast as a man.

It has a foot-long upright tail, long power-packed legs, and short rounded wings.

90

Bald Eagle

THE Bald Eagle is not really bald. It has white head feathers to match its white tail feathers. But its large body, its great wings, and strong legs are covered with dark brown feathers, so that from a distance it actually looks bald.

This great American bird, with its big eight-foot wing spread, lives high up on rocky cliffs. With its keen eyesight, it can watch the surface of rivers and lakes far below. From its high perch, it can swoop down upon fish, waterfowl, or upon rabbits racing for cover. With its huge, sharp talons it can scoop up these animals and carry them up to its nest.

Prothonotary Warbler

In England, many years ago, there was a kind of Chief Clerk of the courts. This man was called a Prothonotary. He wore a bright yellow hood. It seems like a big name to have given a sweet, little Warbler, just because it, too, has a golden yellow head.

Red-Headed Woodpecker

The Red-Headed Woodpecker has been called the Carpenter Bird because it spends a lot of time drilling into trees with its strong, sharp-edged bill. When you see a Woodpecker drilling into a tree, it is either making a nest or looking for insect eggs that make up its food.

Cardinal

THIS rich red, crested, black-faced bird gets its name from the color of the robes worn by a cardinal of the Roman Catholic Church. It makes its home in any area that has thickets and tangles near open spaces.

It will eat insects and fruits but its favorite foods are the seeds of sunflowers, melons, and squash. When people place such seeds where wandering Cardinals can get at them, these birds become regular residents of the locality. They repay these human favors with their rich, loud and happy singing.

93

Albatross

THE great white Albatross is not only the largest water bird, but in some ways the largest flying bird in the world. Though not as large of body as the mighty condor, its wing spread is 14 feet, which is as large as a small two-seated airplane.

The Albatross nests on high land overlooking the sea, but spends most of its time flying far out over the ocean. It can fly thousands of miles and fast enough to keep up with an ocean liner. For days it will follow a steamer. Each day when the garbage is thrown out at the stern, the Albatross will scoop up and eat whatever floats on the water. It can be tamed quite easily. For this reason, lonely sailors have grown very fond of the Albatross. They will tell you it is very bad luck to kill one.

Cormorant

THE Cormorant is a big, black bird with a white or yellow face. Cormorants live along the world's seashores.

In Chinese and Japanese waters, they have been trained to catch fish for man. A ring of hemp (of which we make rope) is tied around the bird's neck so that it is unable to swallow. Thus prevented from eating the fish, the Cormorant carries it in its bill to the boat of its owner and drops it in the boat. When the boat is full, the ring is taken off and the Cormorant is rewarded with fish for itself.

Penguin

THE Penguin lives in the far south of the world around the South Pole. It

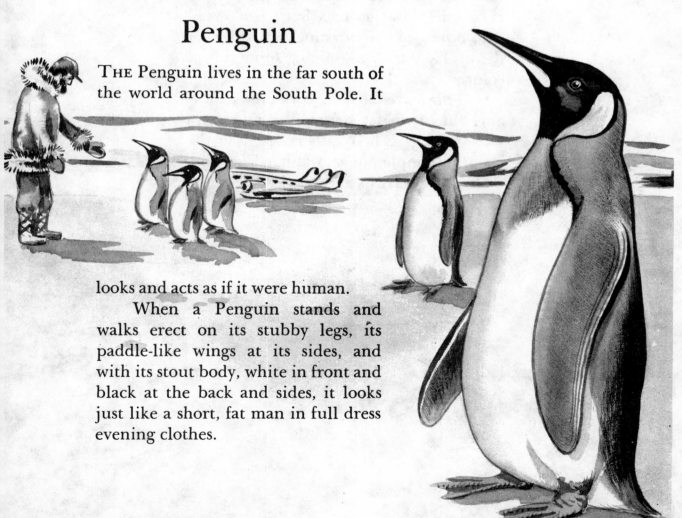

looks and acts as if it were human.

When a Penguin stands and walks erect on its stubby legs, its paddle-like wings at its sides, and with its stout body, white in front and black at the back and sides, it looks just like a short, fat man in full dress evening clothes.

Bird of Paradise

IT is truly, the Birds of Paradise, for in and around the big island of New Guinea, in the South Seas, there are more than 40 different kinds of these unbelievably beautiful birds. Not only do these birds have beautiful, rich colors on their feathery bodies, but they have extra feathers of still other colors bursting out all over them. They look like living fountains of color.

They have tails like corkscrews, movable shields of feathery color, and extra sets of wings. Their calls range from the clang of temple gongs to a harsh scream. They live on fruits and berries.

Whip-Poor-Will

THE Whip-Poor-Will is colored brownish with a few white markings. The odd thing about the Whip-Poor-Will is that nearly everyone has heard it but hardly anyone has ever seen it. That is because it sleeps all day and lives and travels by night.

It does not build a nest, like other birds, but lays its eggs on a pile of dead leaves on the ground. At night and especially before a storm, it can be heard calling on the world to "whip-poor-will," in tones so sad, that once heard you will never forget them.

Chimney Swift

THIS little bird with narrow, slightly curved wings, and not much tail, really lives up to its name. It is the fastest living thing that flies. It can go 100 miles an hour. It has been known to cover 1,000 miles in a single day.

Then, too, it likes to roost in unused chimneys. It feeds on the many small flying insects that fill the air in summertime.

Spoonbill

THE Spoonbill is one of the funniest looking birds. But it is also one of the most beautiful. It has a white breast, but the rest of it is a wonderful shade of rose.

It gets its name from its silly bill which looks just like a very large spoon held in its mouth, with the bowl end out. This silly looking thing is one of the most practical eating machines in Nature. With it the Spoonbill is able to scoop up shrimps and crabs and other shell fish that it cannot even see in muddy waters.

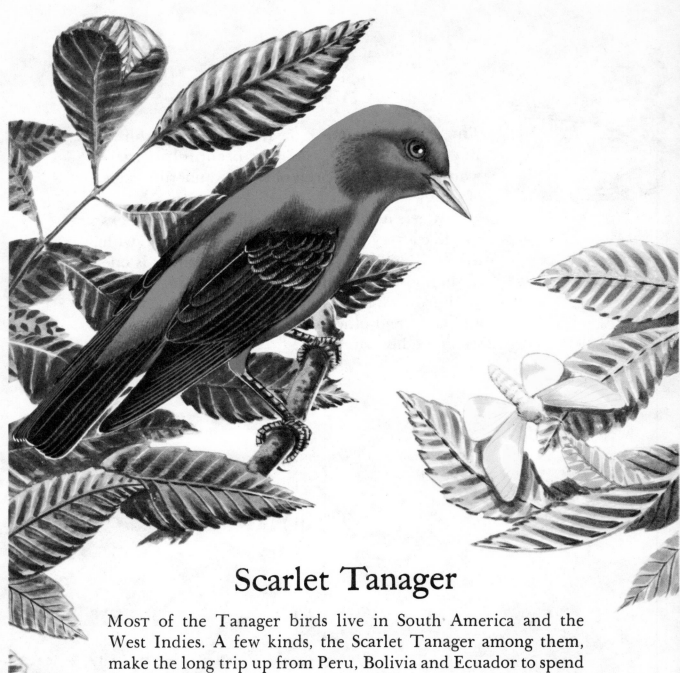

Scarlet Tanager

Most of the Tanager birds live in South America and the West Indies. A few kinds, the Scarlet Tanager among them, make the long trip up from Peru, Bolivia and Ecuador to spend their summers in the United States.

The Scarlet Tanager is the most widely known of the Tanagers. It is colored a gorgeous vivid red, and is the most brilliant of all our northern birds. You may have heard it called the "Firebird."

In our country this beautiful bird was almost killed off by men who sold its feathers to make women's hats. Laws were passed to stop this killing and one of our loveliest song birds was saved.

100

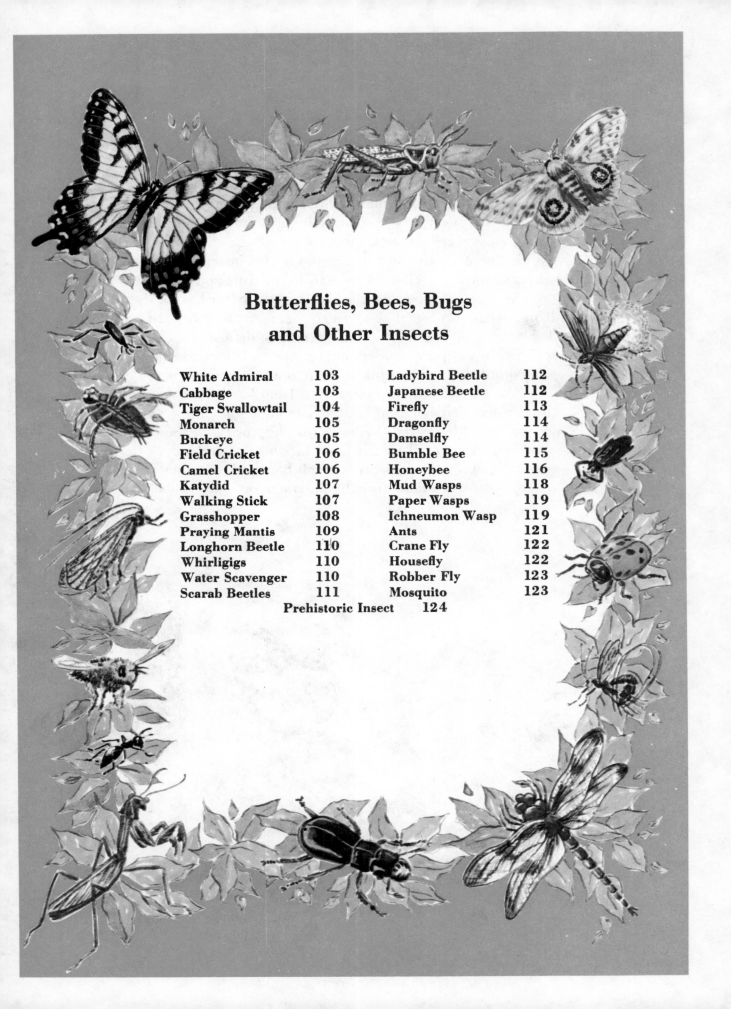

Butterflies, Bees, Bugs
and Other Insects

W E all know that butterflies, bees and bugs are insects. But have you ever wondered just what an insect *is*? Many people wonder whether or not an insect is an animal. An insect is very definitely an animal. As a matter of fact, insects are the most numerous of all the animals in the world. There are also more different kinds of insects than there are of all the other kinds of animals in the world put together.

An insect can be identified by the fact that it has six legs. It never has two legs, like a human being, or four legs, like a dog or a horse. Nor does it ever have more than six legs, like a spider or a centipede. Spiders and centipedes belong to a closely related order of animals but they are not true insects.

Another way you can tell insects from other animals is by the peculiar shape of their bodies. The bodies of all insects are joined into three parts: the head, the chest or *thorax*, and the abdomen. Almost all insects have *antennae* or feelers. These may be long or short, pointed or club-shaped, but they stick out of an insect's head like the antennae on a television set.

White Admiral

MOST butterflies like to fly about in wide open, sunny spaces. The White Admiral prefers the forest, and you will find this butterfly darting in and out of woods and along shaded paths. White Admirals are colored white, red and black.

Cabbage

CABBAGE Butterflies can be found almost anywhere, but especially where there are vegetable plants. You might think that Cabbage Butterflies like to eat a lot. The curious thing is that butterflies never eat a thing; they just sip juices. It is only when they are in the *larva* or infant caterpillar state that they eat, and then they eat a tremendous lot.

103

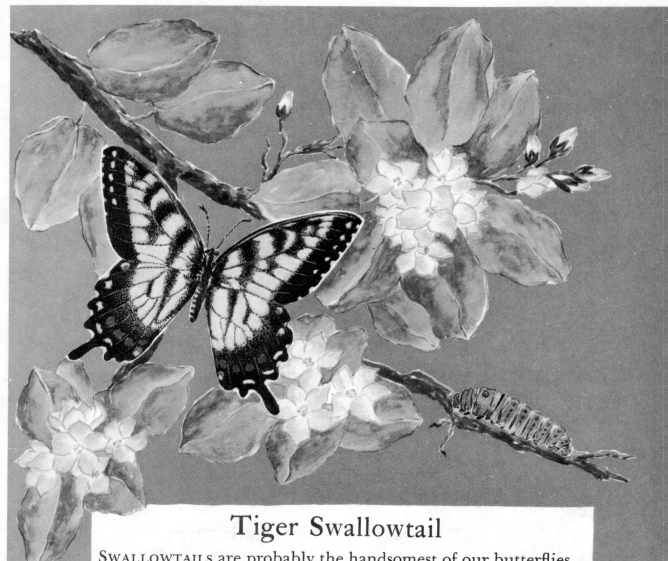

Tiger Swallowtail

SWALLOWTAILS are probably the handsomest of our butterflies. There is no doubt that they are the largest. You can easily spot a Swallowtail by its great size and by the tail-like parts of its hindwings. The Tiger Swallowtail has yellow wings with black stripes, like a tiger's coat.

All butterflies face the danger of being eaten alive by birds, especially when they are in the caterpillar state. Nature has a wonderful way of protecting the Swallowtail caterpillar. The front of its tiny green body has two big round yellow spots which look like the eyes of a snake. And hidden in its head are two orange horns which resemble a snake's forked tongue. These horns suddenly shoot out when the caterpillar is frightened. Birds think they have come upon a snake and are frightened away.

Monarch

By far the favorite American butterfly is the orange and black Monarch. Of all butterflies, this one is certainly the most accomplished traveller.

In the fall Monarchs gather in great swarms to start their famous migration to the south.

Buckeye

The Buckeye is a born fighter. This butterfly of medium size will pick a fight with larger butterflies, and it will even pit its strength against big grasshoppers or birds.

The upper spots on the hindwings of the Buckeye are so large and staring that they look like the eyes of a buck deer, which is how this little scrapper got its name.

Field Cricket

CRICKETS are the musicians of the insect world. Their cheerful chirps are really mating calls. Only the male crickets make music. The females find their mates by listening for the serenades of the males.

Have you ever wondered how crickets make their music? The veins on their front wings are very thick and along their hind legs are tiny ridges. The sounds come when the ridges of the hind legs are scraped against the wings, somewhat the way a violinist draws the bow along the strings of a fiddle. This insect's ears are situated, of all places, on the shins of its forelegs!

Camel Cricket

WE do not need anyone to tell us why this hump-backed insect is called the Camel Cricket. It is especially fond of damp places, and you can usually find it under the stones and logs in cellars and caves.

Katydid

WHEN you hear the familiar "Katy did, Katy she did, she did," you can be sure it is a male Katydid singing. But he is no tattle tale, for that is all he ever says about her.

Katydids do not really sing, of course. Like all insects, they do not possess such a thing as a voice. To sing out "Katydid," the male rubs his wings together three times; to say "she did," he rubs them twice.

Walking Stick

THIS insect could not be better named. It looks exactly like a stick that walks and when it is not moving you would be certain to mistake it for a stick or twig. This is one more example of Nature's marvelous way of protecting her own.

The color of the Walking Stick changes with the seasons. It is green when the leaves are green, during the spring, and when the leaves turn brown in the fall so does the color of the Walking Stick.

Grasshopper

GRASSHOPPERS belong to the same chirping family as crickets and katydids. They are the acrobats of the family. A blade of grass makes a fine trapeze for the Grasshopper. With its long hind legs and strong muscles it can leap far into the air. It uses its wings to glide gracefully back to the ground.

It is not easy to catch Grasshoppers. If you have ever tried you probably found that they shot "tobacco juice" at you. This "tobacco juice," which Grasshoppers spit out of their mouths, is dark brown and it has a bad smell, thus keeping the Grasshopper's enemies away.

Grasshoppers make their chirping sounds by rubbing their hind legs together. Only male Grasshoppers chirp though; and the silence of the females has led to this saying:

"Happy are the Grasshoppers' lives
They all have noiseless wives"

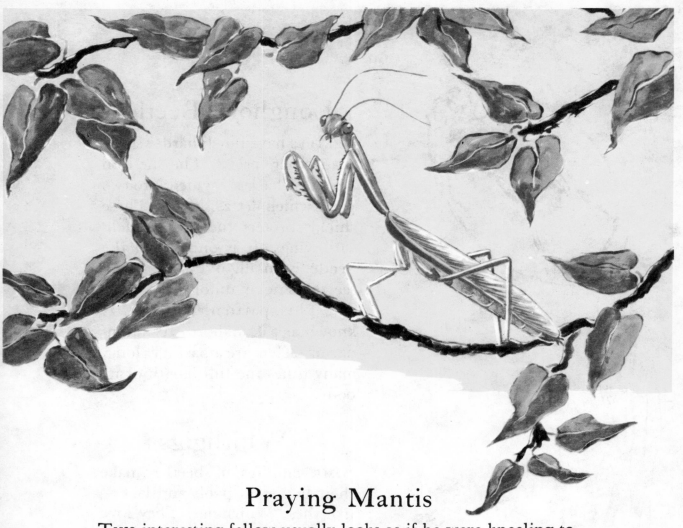

Praying Mantis

THIS interesting fellow usually looks as if he were kneeling to say his prayers before going to bed. That is the typical way he stands, and that of course is how he got his name of Praying Mantis. But do not let his peaceful looks fool you. He is a ferocious fighter, feared even by insects many times his size. You might call him the hobgoblin of the insect world. With his powerful front legs he can crush an enemy to death in an instant. But because he kills so many different kinds of destructive agricultural pests, he is known as the farmer's best insect friend.

You can make a wonderful pet of the Praying Mantis. You can train him to drink water out of a teaspoon and to eat chopped meat from a saucer. After every meal he will wash his face, just like a cat does with its front paws. From his corner he will follow your every move, his head cocked perkily to one side, like a playful puppy.

109

Longhorn Beetle

BEETLES have much harder shells than other insects. The shell on a beetle's back is divided into two parts which act as shields. These shields protect the beetle's delicate wings. It is only when the beetle is in flight that you can see the shields unfold.

This particular beetle is known as a Longhorn. Its antennae or feelers are amazingly long, many times the full length of its body.

Whirligigs

SOME families of beetles make their homes in pools and lakes—like these Whirligigs. They love to swim in groups.

Whirligigs get their name from the way they go whirligigging about in circles, twirling around and around, like we do when we dance the jig or polka.

Water Scavenger

THE savage Water Scavenger preys upon all forms of life that inhabit the world of pools and lakes. Unlike Whirligigs, it enjoys the land as much as the water. It is especially attracted to electric lights.

Scarab Beetles

THERE are many families of Scarab Beetles. One is the well-known "tumblebug." Its name comes from the clumsy way it rolls the dung of cows and horses into round balls.

Another type of Scarab is the Unicorn. On the top of this page is a picture of a male Unicorn in flight. You can see from this picture how the protective covering of a beetle unfolds into two shields when it is flying. Still another member of the Scarab family is the Stag Beetle, so called because its jaws look something like the antlers of a male deer or stag.

111

Ladybird Beetle

You probably know these small, spotted beetles by their nickname of "ladybugs." Did you know that they are perhaps our most valuable insects? The reason is that Ladybird Beetles love to eat mealy bugs and mealy bugs are terrible pests.

Japanese Beetle

In contrast to the helpful Ladybird, this beetle is one of our worst insect enemies.

Adult Japanese Beetles eat the foliage and fruit of a large variety of plants, while their young damage the roots by sucking the juice out of them.

Firefly

FIREFLIES are the fairy lamplighters of the insect world. They can turn their lights on and off whenever they want to, just as we would use a battery flashlight. But Fireflies do not use their lights for the same purpose we do, to see their way at night. Their lights are mating signals.

The female of this strange member of the beetle family does not have wings and she cannot fly in the air. When it is dark the female Firefly crawls up on a high blade of grass where she waits for the flashing signals of male Fireflies passing over-head. Then she blinks her own lights on and off, so that one of the males will see her signals and fly down to mate with her.

Dragonfly and Damselfly

THESE insects have the wings of airplanes and they speed through the air and swoop down upon their prey like mighty bombardiers on the attack. The Dragonfly is larger than its near relative the Damselfly. It is also a stronger flier. Dragonflies can zoom through the air at a mile a minute, making them the fastest insects known.

You may have heard the Dragonfly spoken of as "the devil's darning needle." It is also supposed to sew up the mouths of naughty children. These are superstitions, of course.

The best way to tell a Dragonfly from a Damselfly is when they are standing still. The Dragonfly always rests with its wings outstretched, whereas the Damselfly keeps its wings close together when not in flight.

Bumble Bee

THE furry bee up at the right of this page is a queen Bumble Bee. You can be sure that all the Bumble Bees you see flying about in the fall will be queens just like her. For each one you see will be the lone survivor of a large colony of Bumble Bees, and each one will be looking for some spot to spend a lonely winter.

All winter long the queen Bumble Bee will stay by herself. She will not come out of her retreat until spring, when she will start to search for a snug hole in the ground, preferably an abandoned mouse nest, which she will make into a home of her own. She will carefully line the sides of the nest with dried bits of leaves and grass. Then she will gather pollen and nectar from flowers. When at last she has stored up a sufficient quantity of food she will lay her eggs.

When these eggs have hatched and grown into a great colony of Bumble Bees, they will include a number of females or queen bees like herself. Except for these queens, the entire colony will perish when cold weather comes.

Honeybee

Is there anything more fascinating in the whole insect world than a Honeybee hive? It is a manufacturing center, a nursery, and a queen's palace.

Every hive is a community made up of thousands upon thousands of individual bees. Like people, different bees do different kinds of work, which is why Honeybees are called *social* insects. The most important member of this bee community is the great queen bee. In size she is bigger and longer than the others. She also lives longer than all the rest. Her task is to lay eggs and she performs her task amazingly well. During a queen bee's life — she lives about three years — she may lay as many as a million eggs!

Wherever the queen bee goes she is always followed by a special group of bees who feed and take care of her. These bees who form the queen's royal court are called worker bees. They even clean and comb the queen's beautiful shining coat.

In addition to the queen and the worker bees, there is a third kind called drones. They are idle, clumsy fellows who never do anything at all except mate with the queen.

Worker bees are the most numerous group of bees in any hive and it is they who do practically all the work. While some take care of the queen, others are kept busy at housework, and still others are nursemaids who tend to the hive's nursery. Each of the queen's many eggs is hatched in a separate room or *cell*. The nursemaid bees keep these cells immaculately clean, and they bathe and feed the baby bees. It is also the worker bees you see flying from flower to flower in the summer months as they gather pollen and nectar which they change into honey. A great deal of this honey is made inside the hive itself. The honey we eat is what is left over after the bees have finished feeding themselves. Fortunately for us, Honeybees make much more honey than they need.

Mud Wasps

THESE wasps make their homes of mud and clay. They have been using these building materials for millions of years, long before man got the idea of using clay bricks to make houses. The Potter Wasp builds beautifully proportioned nests of clay that look like small jugs or vases.

Mason Wasps prefer underground holes but sometimes they hang their nests from the branches of trees. And you will usually find the nests of the thin-waisted Mud Dauber Wasps in attics or barns.

Paper Wasps

NOT all wasps build their homes of clay. Some use paper, and those that do may be truly called the world's oldest papermakers. They make the paper for their nests by chomping on bits of wood until it becomes a pasty pulp.

We have learned to make paper in much the same way, except that we use machines. Among the many families of Paper Wasps are the Yellowjackets.

Ichneumon Wasp

A CURIOUS relative of the wasp family is the Ichneumon. The female lays eggs in the strangest places. What seems to be her long curled up tail is not a tail at all but a sharply pointed hollow tube. She uses it to pierce through several inches of tree trunk to drop her eggs in places where there will be food when the eggs hatch.

119

Ants

IF you have ever disturbed an ant colony, perhaps by turning over a stone under which ants were living, you may have seen them rushing about in every which way. You may have wondered about the reason for all this frantic hurrying, what it was they were carrying between their jaws, and where they were going when they suddenly disappeared into the ground.

Ants are the most highly developed of the social insects. By *social*, of course, we mean that they have developed the habit of living together, as in families or communities. Every ant community has its queen, a number of kings or males, and a great many workers. Some even have a special class of warriors or soldiers. The important thing is that each member of an ant colony has some special task to perform.

Individual ants do not work for themselves alone but for the good of their fellows. Thus, the ants you saw when you overturned the stone were probably worker ants. They were scurrying about with little *pupae* in their jaws, infant ants, which they were carrying away to safety in their underground communities.

Crane Fly

THE insects on this page and the next are all true flies. They have a single pair of wings, which is what distinguishes them from other types of flying insects. The long-legged fly on the left is the Crane Fly, often mistaken for the "daddy long-legs."

Housefly

You know that Houseflies are dangerous because they can carry the germs of diseases. But do you know how they carry germs?

This is how. The Housefly feeds by sucking, and so solid bits of food must always be softened before they can be digested. To do that the Housefly lets out a drop of liquid from its mouth onto the food and then sucks some of it back in. If we leave food uncovered, especially during the hot summer months when Houseflies are numerous, the food can be contaminated by these drops of liquid.

Robber Fly

THE big, hairy Robber Fly, with eyes that bulge, will pounce upon an insect flying in midair. Its legs form a basket which it uses to capture its prey while still in flight. Another name for this fly is the Assassin Fly.

Mosquito

YOU will never be bitten by a male Mosquito. Only female Mosquitos bite. And the only reason they ever bite is that at least once in their lifetime they must suck the blood of some warm-blooded animal before their eggs will develop properly. The larvae of Mosquitos are called "wrigglers," and they breed in ponds and pools.

Prehistoric Insect

THIS strange creature is believed to be the biggest insect that ever lived. Its wing measurements are two feet from tip to tip and the body alone is 15 inches long.

Archaeologists discovered the insect imbedded in stone where it had been preserved for millions and millions of years.

124

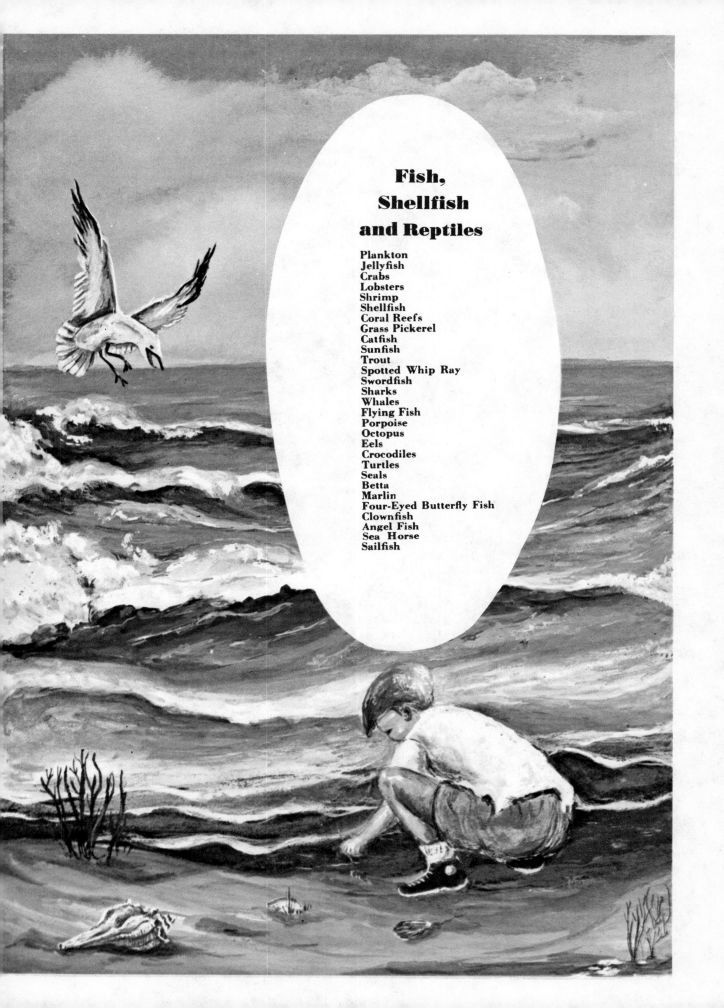

Fish, Shellfish and Reptiles

Plankton
Jellyfish
Crabs
Lobsters
Shrimp
Shellfish
Coral Reefs
Grass Pickerel
Catfish
Sunfish
Trout
Spotted Whip Ray
Swordfish
Sharks
Whales
Flying Fish
Porpoise
Octopus
Eels
Crocodiles
Turtles
Seals
Betta
Marlin
Four-Eyed Butterfly Fish
Clownfish
Angel Fish
Sea Horse
Sailfish

Have you ever stood by the edge of the sea and looked out over the endless waters that stretch way off into the horizon, and beyond? "How pretty," you must have thought as you watched the sun's rays dance merrily on this great blanket of water.

If only you were able to see through this blanket, down deep into the water, you would see sights such as you never thought existed. For just below this blanket of blue, there lives in the sea a silent world, a world of beauty, mystery, and sometimes danger.

With our new and better underwater breathing equipment, more and more of us have been able to go into this strange, silent world.

As the brave men who explore our ocean world return, they bring with them the pictures and stories of the things they have seen. As you turn the pages of this section, you will be able to share in some of the secrets and beauty of the fish, shellfish, and amphibians that live in our undersea world.

Plankton

OUR oceans are full of tiny animals called Plankton. Even though Plankton are no larger than specks of dust they are an important food for many of the fish that live in the sea.

Jellyfish

JELLYFISH are among the simplest creatures that live in the sea. There are many kinds of Jellyfish. Some of them have clear bodies that look like glass. Others have a pink or orange color. Some Jellyfish shine in the dark.

Along our shores we may find Jellyfish that are no bigger than a half dollar. In the ocean there are pink Jellyfish that grow as big as the top of a barrel. The larger Jellyfish, in the picture on this page, is a pink Jellyfish.

The smaller Jellyfish, in the picture on this page, is a Portuguese Man-of-War. The Man-of-War has tentacles that contain a deadly poison. When a fish is stung by this poison it becomes paralyzed. The Man-of-War's poison is also dangerous to man, and the slightest sting can cause great pain.

Crabs

Most Crabs make their homes in rocks and seaweed under the sea. All Crabs walk sideways, and when they grow too big for their shell, they grow a new one.

Crab-meat is good to eat. The Crab shown on the top of the page is a Market Crab. Market Crabs have much meat and are an important food for man.

Lobsters

A LOBSTER is more like a spider than a fish. Like a spider, the Lobster walks on its many long thin legs. In the front of its body are two large claws that are used to catch and crush food.

Most of the Lobsters that we eat come from the ocean waters near Maine and lower Canada.

Shrimp

SHRIMP look like small lobsters without claws. They live near sandy beaches all over the world. Shrimp hide from their enemies by covering themselves with loose wet sand. Shrimp make tasty food.

Shellfish

ON the side of this page are popular shellfish animals. From top to bottom they are: the Snail, the Hermit Crab, the Scallop, and the Oyster. All these animals grow their own shells except the Hermit Crab.

131

Coral Reefs

IN our southern seas there are many mountains that are miles long and hundreds of feet high. These mountains are made of Coral. The Coral is a small animal that lives in the warm waters of the tropics. There are many kinds of Coral, and they all have beautiful colors.

When Coral die they leave a hard skeleton for other Coral to live on. The Coral stick together and pile on top of each other until great mountains of Coral are made. These mountains of Coral are called Coral Reefs. Some of these Coral Reefs are millions of years old.

Sometimes these Coral Reefs grow so high that their tops stick out of the water and become small islands. Coral Reefs can be dangerous to man. If a ship crashes into a hidden reef it may be wrecked.

Under the sea many fish make their homes in the small caves that are found in Coral Reefs. Wherever there is Coral many fish and plenty of food can always be found.

Grass Pickerel

GRASS Pickerel live in lakes and quiet streams. They like to make their homes in shallow water where there are weeds and a muddy bottom.

The Grass Pickerel is a small fish and often people mistake it for a baby northern pike.

As a sport or game fish, the Grass Pickerel is not very important because of its small size.

Catfish

CATFISH are among the most popular fish in America. There are many different kinds of Catfish living in our fresh water lakes and streams.

Most Catfish like warm muddy waters. They will eat almost anything that they find on the muddy bottom.

All Catfish have small eyes and long feelers that look like a cat's whiskers. Unlike most other fish, Catfish have no scales.

Catfish are very hardy and can live out of water longer than most fish. Many people like to eat Catfish.

Sunfish

THE little Sunfish is one of the most popular fresh water fish in the United States. There are many different kinds of Sunfish living in our streams and lakes. Most of these fish are only three to eight inches long. Sunfish have bright blue, yellow, and orange colored skins.

These fish are always plentiful and are easy to catch on a small hook baited with a worm. Even though they are small they make a tasty meal.

Trout

SPORTSMEN have fished for Trout since the days when America was first settled.

Most Trout live in cool, rushing streams. They eat insects, worms, and other small fish.

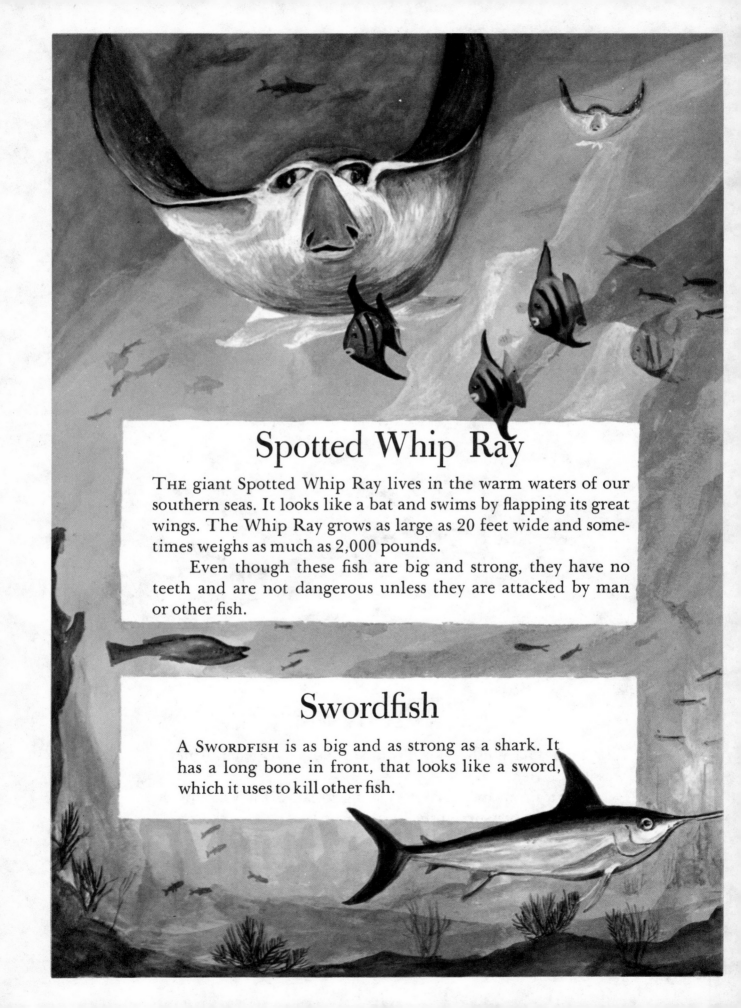

Spotted Whip Ray

THE giant Spotted Whip Ray lives in the warm waters of our southern seas. It looks like a bat and swims by flapping its great wings. The Whip Ray grows as large as 20 feet wide and sometimes weighs as much as 2,000 pounds.

Even though these fish are big and strong, they have no teeth and are not dangerous unless they are attacked by man or other fish.

Swordfish

A SWORDFISH is as big and as strong as a shark. It has a long bone in front, that looks like a sword, which it uses to kill other fish.

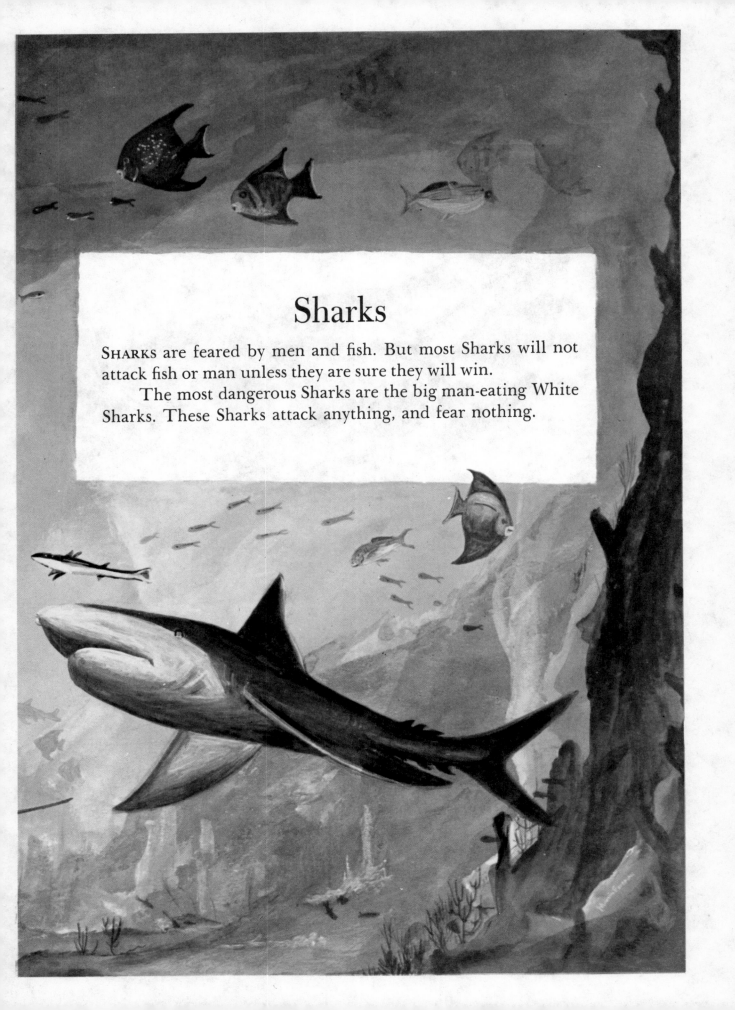

Sharks

SHARKS are feared by men and fish. But most Sharks will not attack fish or man unless they are sure they will win.

The most dangerous Sharks are the big man-eating White Sharks. These Sharks attack anything, and fear nothing.

Whales

WHALES, the largest animals in the world, spend all their lives in the water, like fish, but they really are not fish. Whales are mammals. A mammal is an animal that has hair and warm blood. All mammals take care of their children. Dogs, cats and cows are mammals that live on land. Can you think of others?

Unlike fish, Whales must breathe air, and cannot stay under the water for more than 20 or 30 minutes.

Sperm Whales, like the one you see in the picture above, are valuable for the oil they carry in the top of their heads. Man uses this oil to make soap and perfume.

138

Flying Fish

THE Flying Fish does not really fly, but it can glide hundreds of feet through the air. This small fish, although never more than 12 inches long, has very large fins that look like wings. When the fish jumps out of the water it spreads its fins and glides over the waves like a bird.

Porpoise

PORPOISE are mammals like the whales. Porpoise always swim in large schools. They can swim very fast and they often jump out of the water high into the air. Porpoise have sharp teeth which they use to fight sharks.

Porpoise are very smart and can be taught to do many tricks. They are friendly animals who love to have fun and to show off.

Octopus

THE Octopus is an ugly monster that lives among the rocks on the bottom of the sea. It has eight strong arms and a mouth that looks like a parrot's beak. When an Octopus is attacked, it will wrap its arms around its enemy and pull it to the bottom of the sea.

Eels

EVEN though the Eel looks like a snake it is a true fish. All Eels are born far out at sea. They swim thousands of miles until they reach inland streams. When the Eel is ready to spawn it returns to the sea where it was born.

Crocodiles

CROCODILES are amphibious reptiles that can live on land and in water. Crocodiles are found in tropical countries all over the world. They like to make their homes near sluggish rivers or open swamps.

Crocodiles have webbed feet which help them walk easily on soft wet ground. Crocodiles feed on small animals and fish, which they swallow whole. Sometimes a Crocodile will attack a large animal or even a man.

Crocodiles lay eggs. They bury their eggs under sand or in nests of weeds and plants. The female Crocodile guards the nest until she can hear her babies grunt. Then she digs the babies out of the nest.

Crocodiles are important to man. They have a tough skin which is made into leather for shoes, handbags, and traveling bags. We make perfume from the oil in their glands.

141

Turtles

THE Sea Turtle is born on land but its life is spent in the sea. When the mother Sea Turtle is ready to lay her eggs she leaves the sea and climbs onto some sandy beach. On the beach she finds a safe place away from the water, and digs a hole in the sand. After burying her eggs in the sand the mother Turtle, who is now very tired, slowly crawls back into the sea. She will never see her children. Soon the eggs hatch and the baby Turtles go down to the sea where they will spend the rest of their lives.

On the top of this page is a picture of a Hawksbill Turtle. The shell of this Turtle is used to make beautiful tortoise-shell combs and jewelry.

The picture just above is that of the Green Turtle. This Turtle can grow to be over four feet long and weigh more than 500 pounds. This big Turtle is used to make Turtle soup.

142

Seals

THE Seal is an air-breathing mammal. Even though the Seal spends part of its time on land, its real home is the sea. There the Seal is a graceful animal, but on land it is clumsy and awkward. Whenever there is danger the Seal rushes to the safety of the sea.

In the picture below, on the left, is a Sea Lion. Sea Lions are the smartest members of the Seal family. Most of the performing circus Seals are Sea Lions.

The Sea Elephant on the right is the largest member of the Seal family.

Betta

THE Betta is a small, tropical, fresh-water fish that is never longer than three inches.

Whenever two male Bettas meet there is a great battle, and they fight to kill. When fighting with a male, or breeding with a female, the male Betta spreads his fins like an ostrich and shows off his beautiful colors. Because of their great beauty, these small fighting fish are bred and kept in aquariums by people all over the world.

Marlin

STRIPED Marlin are found only in the Pacific Ocean. They are huge fish that weigh 600 pounds or more.

It is thrilling to see this fish streak through the water at top speed and then leap high into the air. The Marlin is famous as a game fish because of the great fight it puts up when it is caught on a fisherman's hook.

Four-Eyed Butterfly Fish

This little fish lives in the waters of the West Indies. It is a very colorful fish and very popular among tropical fish lovers all over the world. This fish got its name because of the large black spot that it has on each side of its back fin. The spot looks like another eye.

Clownfish

One of the greatest enemies of small fish is the sea anemone. The sea anemone looks like a flower, but it has long, waving tentacles that are full of poison.

For some strange reason, the sea anemone does not harm the Clownfish. Whenever this funny looking fish is threatened by danger, it swims in among the anemone's tentacles where other fish are afraid to follow.

Angel Fish

The Angel Fish is one of the most colorful fish found near coral reefs.

It has a flat, brightly striped body that shines in the water as it swims lazily along.

This fish is called an Angel Fish not only for its beauty, but because its fins look like wings.

146

Sea Horse

THE Sea Horse is a strange looking creature. It is a true fish, but it swims in an upright position and has no tail fin.

Like all other fish, it breathes through gills which are on both sides of its head. Its body is covered by tiny scales that join together to make a hard suit of armor.

One of the strangest things about the Sea Horse is that the father has the babies instead of the mother. The father has a pouch like a kangaroo. The mother puts her eggs in this pouch and then goes on her way, leaving the father to hatch the eggs. When the eggs are hatched, about 200 baby Sea Horses swim out of the father's body.

Most Sea Horses are only three or four inches long. They are found along the shores of most tropical seas.

Sailfish

SAILFISHING is an exciting sport enjoyed by many people. The Sailfish lives in the Atlantic and Pacific Oceans. When it is caught on a fisherman's hook, it will leap high out of the water and fight ferociously to get the hook loose.

The Sailfish is not very good to eat because its meat is very oily. Fishermen like to stuff and display this beautiful fish in their homes.

Flowers and Plants

Garden Flowers	**Gladiolus**
Iris	**Poppy**
Rose	**Aster**
Lady-Slipper	**Chrysanthemum**
Crocus	**Buttercup**
Lily-of-the-Valley	**Dutchman's Breeches**
Lily	**Honeysuckle**
Pansy	**Venus's-Flytrap**
Bleeding-Heart	**Ferns**
Dahlia	**Carnivorous Flowers**
Sweet Pea	**Useful Plants**
Camellia	**Cotton**
Carnation	**Peanut**
Bachelor's Button	**Peppermint**
Peony	**Parasitic Plants**
Hyacinth	**Orchid**

Every living thing is either animal or plant. Plants can grow up into the air or down into the ground. They cannot go from place to place as animals do. Animals have to move to hunt for food. Plants make the food they need out of sunshine, air, and minerals from the soil.

With a wonderful chemical called chlorophyll, which makes their leaves green, plants manufacture sugar. This sugar is the source of all the food in the world. For animals eat plants or other animals which have eaten plants. So it all goes back to the sugar in the plants.

Trees, shrubs, grasses, vines, and weeds are all plants. Like all living things, plants can reproduce their kind. The flowers make this possible. Just as animals are male or female, so flowers are *staminate* and *pistulate*. The stamens hold the pollen. Deep within the pistils are the ovules or seeds of life.

Nature makes flowers beautiful, gives them a lovely smell, and fills them with honey-sweet nectar so that they will lure the insects. When butterflies, bees, and hummingbirds go from flower to flower gathering nectar, they carry pollen to the seeds. These unite in the miracle of creation.

Garden Flowers

GARDEN flowers are those that we plant, water, weed, fertilize and otherwise take care of ourselves. This is called cultivation. All of our cultivated flowers were once wild flowers.

Flowers we replant each year are called annuals. Perennials are those that will bloom year after year.

Iris

IRIS is so hardy that it will survive the cold of Siberia and also the heat of India. Iris is the Greek word for rainbow, and it comes in all the colors of the rainbow. Blue Flag, a wild Iris, grows in meadows in this country. Iris is the state flower of Tennessee.

Rose

THE most beautiful and best known of our garden flowers is the Rose. There are wild Roses in many of the cooler parts of the world. They have been cultivated for many hundreds of years in China, Persia, and Europe. Cultivated Roses are like domestic cats and dogs. People have cross-bred different kinds of Roses to make new and more beautiful kinds.

The most beautiful of all Roses, the American Beauty Rose, was really an accident. One day some years ago, it appeared in the corner of a garden in Washington, D. C. The bees had mixed up the pollen and seeds of Roses that would have been kept strictly apart if the garden had not been neglected.

153

Lady-Slipper

THE Lady-Slipper, a cousin of the orchid, gets its name because one part of it is shaped like a lady's slipper.

There is a smaller kind that hides away in deeply shaded bogs. It is called the Fairy Slipper. Another, which the Indians called Moccasin Flower, can be replanted and grown in your garden.

Crocus

LIKE the robin, the Crocus tells us that spring is on the way. This tough, little flower pushes up through late snow.

Sometimes it is so white it cannot be seen. But it grows in your favorite colors too. From the orange-streaked flowers of one kind of Crocus comes the coloring used on candy and cakes.

Lily-of-the-Valley

THE Lily-of-the-Valley is a dainty, little member of the lily family. Its blossoms look like nodding, small, white bells. It has a lovely, sweet scent. It grows wild in the woods of Europe and northern Asia. In the United States, it grows in the woods of our eastern mountains.

Lily

THE Lily is a very large family of flowering plants. It includes not only Lilies and lilies-of-the-valley, but also such flowers shown on other pages as iris, hyacinth, tulip, and daffodil. And believe it or not, asparagus, leek, onion and garlic are in the same family as Lilies.

Pansy

PANSY is from the French *pen-sée* which means thought or re-membrance. Pansies have funny little clown faces made by darker markings on light ones.

Bleeding-Heart

THIS pretty flower has heart-shaped, deep pink blossoms and fern-like leaves. You will find the Bleeding-Heart in many gardens.

Dahlia

THE original Dahlia was a small red flower with a yellow center.

Sweet Pea

THE Sweet Pea comes in more different colors than any other flower.

Camellia

THE Camellia Japonica is the beautiful blossom of an evergreen shrub closely related to the tea plant. In the south it is called just Japonica.

Carnation

THE Carnation is probably the most popular flower after the rose. The Red Carnation is the state flower of Ohio. Related pink Carnations grow wild.

Bachelor's Button

IT is said that an unmarried man wears this flower to find out if his girl loves him.

Peony

PEONIES are native to eastern Asia and southern Europe.

157

Hyacinth

THE small blossoms come in blue, purple, lilac, pink, red, or white. They are closely packed in bell-shaped clusters.

When Hyacinths were brought to America in colonial days, a wild Hyacinth grew here. It was so prized by the Indians that when white men trampled a field of them, it started an Indian war.

Gladiolus

THE purple, red, orange, yellow, or white blossoms of the Gladiolus grow on only one side of its long stem facing the sun. The bulbs have to be stored away from frost in warm cellars each fall and replanted in the garden when spring comes.

Poppy

THE Poppy is native to many different lands and climates. The beautiful, golden-yellow Poppy is the state flower of California. The oriental Poppy of Turkey and Armenia is a flaming red with a purple-black center.

159

Aster

ASTERS are among the commonest of wild flowers. There are also many different garden varieties. Most of the wild Asters are blue, lavender, or pinkish. All these have yellow centers. The cultivated Chinese Asters have no yellow center. There is a giant California Aster which grows three feet tall.

160

Chrysanthemum

THE Chinese cultivated the Chrysanthemum more than 2,500 years ago. The Japanese made it their national flower.

Today we raise it in red, purple, yellow, and white. It comes in dainty, little button-hole flowers and in huge eight-inch soft balls on stems four feet long.

Buttercup

THIS little flower looks like a cup and is the color of butter. It has large, green leaves forked like crow's feet and is sometimes called Crow's Feet, too.

There are 40 different kinds of Buttercup in the United States. The giant Buttercup grown in gardens is from China and is called Trollius.

Dutchman's Breeches

THESE white blossoms with yellow centers are shaped like a heart and have feathery, fern-like leaves, but they *do* look like little Dutch boy's pants hanging on a line upside down.

These flowers grow wild from Canada to South Carolina and westward to the Great Plains. They are closely related to the bleeding-heart which came to us all the way from China.

Honeysuckle

THE small, trumpet-shaped Honeysuckle flowers are red outside and deep yellow inside. The lovely trumpets give out no sound, but a heavenly, sweet smell.

Honeysuckle may be either a shrub or a woody climber. This kind will twine its way through the woods or over a porch trellis.

163

Venus's-Flytrap

THE Venus's-Flytrap is a carnivorous plant and grows in the south. It has two trap leaves, one on each side of the flower. These leaves are four inches long.

On the inside surfaces of the leaves are tiny trigger hairs. When an insect steps on two of these hairs, the leaf starts to fold. In less than one second it has snapped shut with the insect locked inside. It takes the leaf a day to digest a small insect, but a week for a big one.

Carnivorous Flowers

CARNIVOROUS means flesh or meat eating. So a carnivorous plant is a plant that eats flesh or meat. This sounds rather strange when we recall that plants are living things that manufacture their own food. Well, these carnivorous plants are nature's exception.

Carnivorous plants are unable to get enough nitrogen from the soil as other plants do. So they have to get nitrogen in the same way you do, by eating things that contain it. But as these plants cannot move to go hunting, they trap insects in strange ways to get their steaks and chops.

Ferns

AMONG plants that have no flowers, the most beautiful are the Ferns. Their bright green leaves grow in a lovely, lacy pattern. Some are so small you can keep them in flower pots at home. But in the tropics they grow as large as trees.

165

Useful Plants

THERE are many flowering plants that are good for more than the beauty of their blossoms. There are herbs that give us peppermint for candy and dill for pickles. There are the plants that give us peanuts, cotton and many other useful things.

Cotton

THE white blossom of the Cotton plant blooms for one day. It leaves a pod called a boll on the end of the stalk, which bursts open a few weeks later. Then the Cotton is ready to pick for the manufacture of thread and cloth.

Peanut

THE Peanut is not a nut at all. It is a tiny vegetable in a pod like a pea. When the pod starts to form, the stem of the Peanut plant turns downward and pushes the pod underground, where it matures so the plant will grow out of the ground again.

166

Peppermint

THIS three-foot high plant is a herb and a member of the mint family. It has a small, pale blue flower. Its oval, shiny leaves are toothed and pointed. They give an oil used to flavor chewing gum, candy and ice cream. In medicine this oil is used to help relieve indigestion, toothache, and, in menthol inhalers, for hay fever and colds. It is also used in ointments to help headache. Michigan produces one half of the world's supply.

Parasitic Plants

PARASITES are plants which attach themselves to other plants and draw food from them. Mistletoe is a typical parasite. The tropical orchid also attaches itself to the bark of trees. But it does not take food from them. It sends its roots into the air from which it gets nourishment.

Orchid

THERE are 10,000 different kinds or species of Orchids. No other plant in the world has so many different species. The most beautiful Orchids are the kinds that are grown in greenhouses and in the tropics.

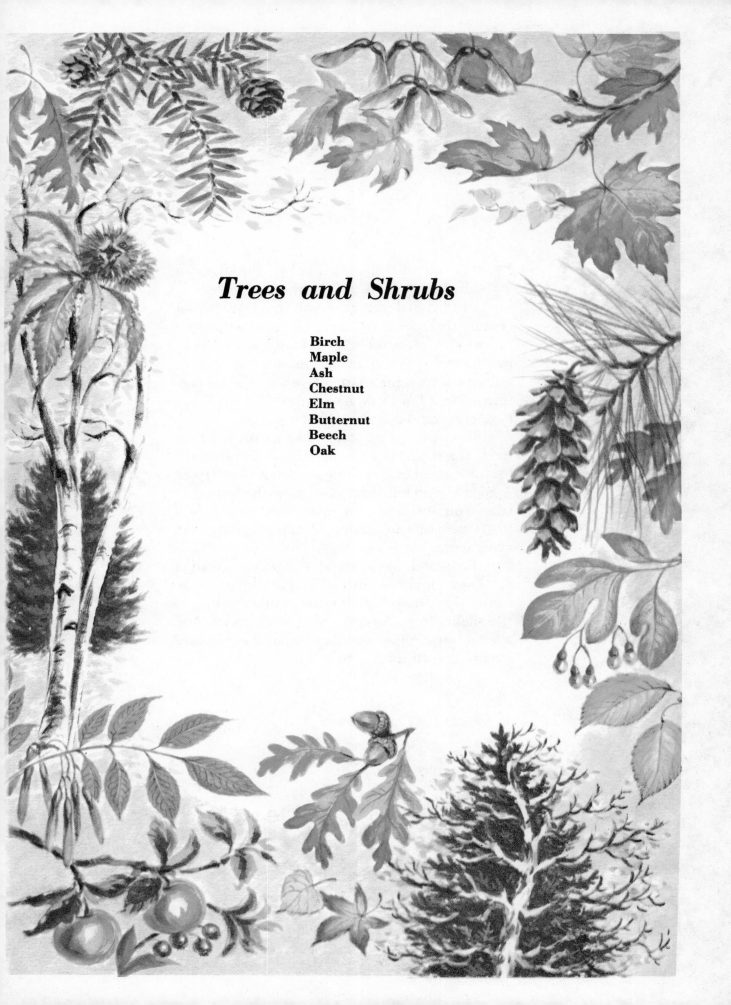

Trees and Shrubs

Birch
Maple
Ash
Chestnut
Elm
Butternut
Beech
Oak

TREES are really plants. They are the largest of all the plants in the world.

Individual trees grow only in one place. But because their seeds are carried by the breezes and the winds, forests of trees actually move. They move forward slowly, a few feet at a time, but in millions of years forests can move across whole continents. In a few cases, like the coconut tree, they have even moved across whole oceans.

Shrubs are plants, too. They are smaller than trees, as a rule. Yet it is sometimes difficult to tell the difference between large shrubs and small trees. A good way to tell them apart is by the form they take. You will find that most trees have only a single stem or trunk, while shrubs generally have many stems.

Trees and shrubs are very important to all of us. They supply us with food. They give us protective shade from the hot summer sun, and protective shelter from the violence of wind storms. And what is just as important, they help make the world a more beautiful place to live in.

Birch

IF you have seen a Birch tree, you know how slender and graceful it is. A variety of Birch tree is called the Paper Birch because
the bark, when peeled off, can be used to write on. The outside
bark is white and marked with lovely charcoal-colored streaks.
The Indians made canoes from the bark of Birch trees,
because it is waterproof. The bark of the Sweet
Birch is dark brown, with lots of short white lines.
From the Sweet Birch comes wintergreen oil.

171

Maple

THE Sugar Maple has a sweet sap which is used to make maple syrup. But this tree has other uses, too. The wood is used for furniture and also for fuel. In the spring there are yellow-green blossoms on the branches of the Maple. Each seed possesses a wing. There are always two seeds joined together so the two wings can be carried by the wind. And from these winged seeds new Maples grow.

The Sugar Maple is but one of about 115 different varieties of Maple. Other popular members of this tree family are the Norway, Oregon, Silver, Moosewood and Japanese Maple.

Ash

STRANGE as it seems, the Ash is a member of the olive tree family.

In the old myths of the Scandinavian peoples, the Ash held a very important place. They believed that the world was supported by a mighty Ash tree, and that it was from an Ash tree that the first man was formed, while the first woman was formed from an Elm tree.

Chestnut

SOME time ago, the Chestnut trees of our Appalachian woods were nearly all killed by a bark disease. Today, young twigs are growing out of the old trunks. Perhaps they will be able to grow into fine trees again. Most of us know how good the nuts are to eat.

Elm

THE American Elm looks like a bursting sky rocket. The trunk splits into branches which grow up and away from the main trunk and then curve suddenly down towards the ground.

Many Elm trees are planted in New England towns along both sides of a street, and the high branches overhang to form a beautiful archway.

174

Butternut

THE leaves of the Butternut tree are light green early in the summer. During the summer they slowly turn yellow. The Butternut tree is found in northern North America all the way west to the Rocky Mountains.

The Butternut is not a strong tree and does not live long. But it does have a delicious tasting nut about one to two inches long. The nut is very pasty, sticking to the branches after the leaves have fallen off.

Beech

THE Beech is a fine shade tree, because its spreading branches have so many thin leaves. The wood is hard and is used for fuel and for lumber. It belongs to the same tree family which includes the chestnuts and the mighty oaks.

In the winter, the trunk of the tree is smooth and gray. In the autumn, nuts fall to the ground from hard, thorny shells. The meat in the nut is very sweet.

175

Oak

YOU may have heard the saying, "From tiny acorns mighty Oak trees grow." These acorns are the nut-like fruit of the Oak trees, and they contain the seeds which grow into new Oak trees. Roasted acorns are good to eat.

There are two main kinds of Oak: the Black Oak and the White Oak. The White Oak is a majestic looking tree. The great strength of its wood makes it excellent for building ships and furniture. The bark of the Black Oak is very dark and its wood is not so strong as the wood of the White Oak.